VISION, SPACE, DESIRE

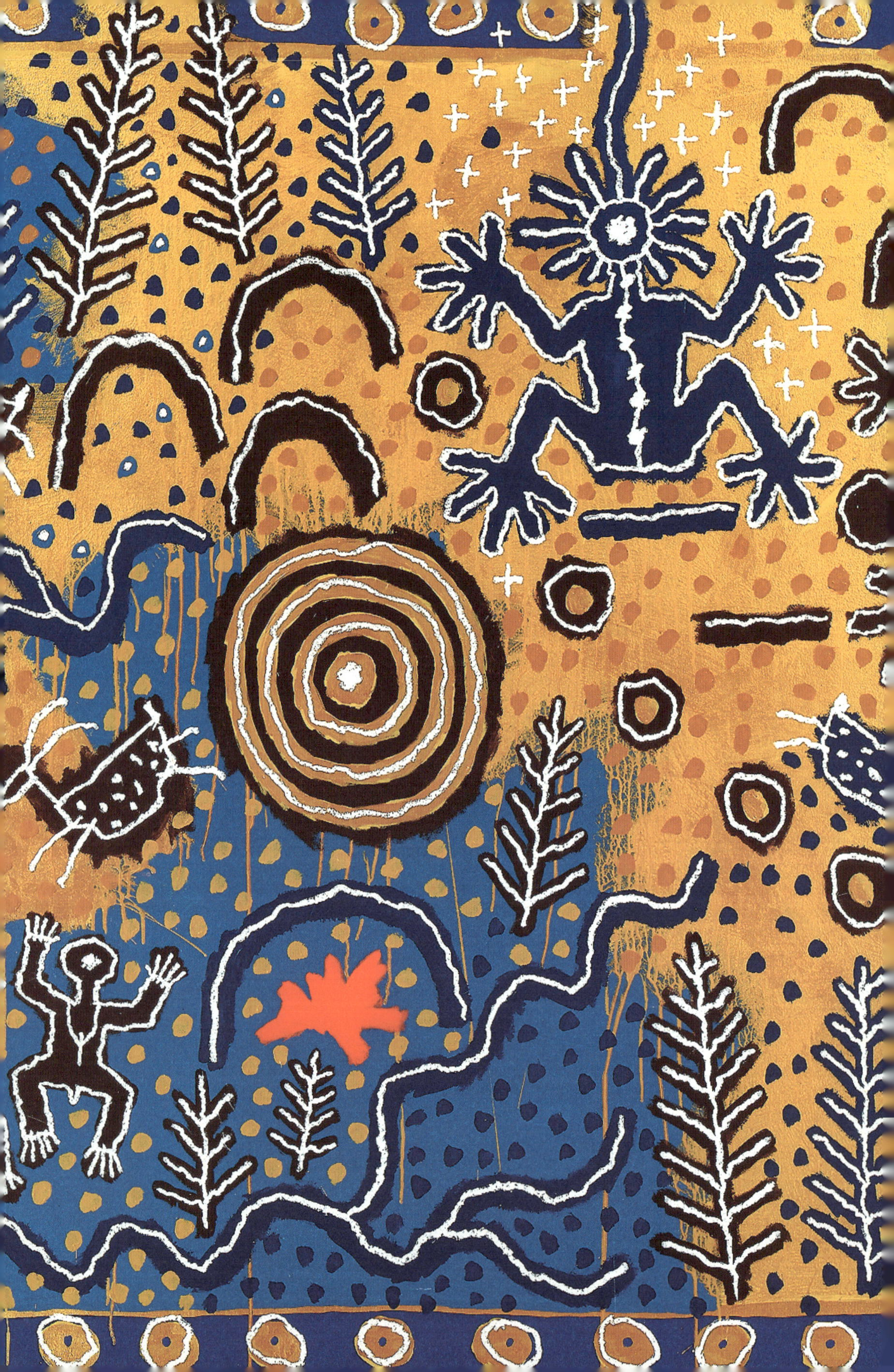

NMAI EDITIONS

VISION, SPACE, DESIRE

Global Perspectives and Cultural Hybridity

National Museum of the American Indian
Smithsonian Institution
Washington, D.C., and New York

Library of Congress Cataloging-in-Publication Data

Vision, space, desire : global perspectives and cultural hybridity.
    p. cm. — (NMAI editions)
Proceedings of a conference held in Venice, Italy, Dec. 2005.
ISBN 978-1-933565-07-1 (alk. paper)
1. Indigenous art—Congresses.
N6351.2.I53V57 2006
704.03'97—dc22
2006039261

Manufactured in the United States of America
The paper used in this publication meets the minimum requirements of the American National Standard for Permanence of Paper for Printed Library Materials Z39.48-1984.

National Museum of the American Indian
Head of Publications: Terence Winch
Editor: Elizabeth Kennedy Gische
Designer: Steve Bell

The Smithsonian's National Museum of the American Indian is dedicated to working in collaboration with the indigenous peoples of the Americas to advance knowledge and understanding of Native cultures throughout the Western Hemisphere. The museum's publishing program seeks to augment awareness of Native American beliefs and lifeways, and to educate the public about the history and significance of Native cultures.

For information about the Smithsonian's National Museum of the American Indian, visit the NMAI website at **www.AmericanIndian.si.edu**. To support the museum by becoming a member, call 1-800-242-NMAI (6624) or click on "Support" on our website.

Title page: Harry Fonseca (Nisenan Maidu/Hawaiian/Portuguese, b. 1946), *Creation 2001* (detail), 2000. Acrylic on canvas, 203 x 542 cm. Collection of the National Museum of the American Indian (26/5007). Photo by Ernest Amoroso. © NMAI.

Table of Contents

10 FOREWORD: At the Table, in the Big Tent
      W. Richard West, Jr.

15 INTRODUCTION: New Art/New Contexts
      Gerald McMaster

31 Delta One Fifty
      Paul Chaat Smith

I. NEW CONTACT ZONES

41 "New Contact Zones": A Reflection
      Jean Fisher

49 Why Venice? Why Visions?
      Salah Hassan

59 The Local and the Global
      Jolene Rickard

69 Meeting, Not Colliding
      Brenda L. Croft

77 A Latin American Perspective
      Ivo Mesquita

85 "Give, Give, Giving": Cultural Translations
      Nancy Marie Mithlo

II. PERFORMING CULTURAL HYBRIDITY

99 Performance and Artistic Mobility
      Lee-Ann Martin

105   A Generative Map
        SYLVIE FORTIN

113   The Third Bank of the River:
        Art and the Indigenous People of Brazil
        PAULO HERKENHOFF

121   Creating Space Within a National Identity
        ROBERT HOULE

127   Doing the Homework
        VASIF KORTUN

133   Te Aö Täwhiti, Te Aö Hou—Old Worlds, New Worlds
        MEGAN TAMATI-QUENNELL

143   Excuse Me While I Kiss the Sky
        JAMES LUNA

III. PERSONAL REFLECTIONS

148   REBECCA BELMORE

151   ANNE ELLEGOOD

154   HARRY FONSECA

156   JEFFREY GIBSON

158   HOCK E AYE VI EDGAR HEAP OF BIRDS

160   SHANNA KETCHUM

164   JASON LUJAN

166   CATHERINE MATTES

170   ALAN MICHELSON

173   JAUNE QUICK-TO-SEE SMITH

176   LORETTA SARAH TODD

Istituto Veneto di Scienze, Lettere ed Arti, Palazzo Cavalli Franchetti, Venice, Italy, site of the National Museum of the American Indian's symposium *Vision, Space, Desire: Global Perspectives and Cultural Hybridity*, December 13, 2005. Photo by Mara Tegon, Comin Foto, Venice. © NMAI.

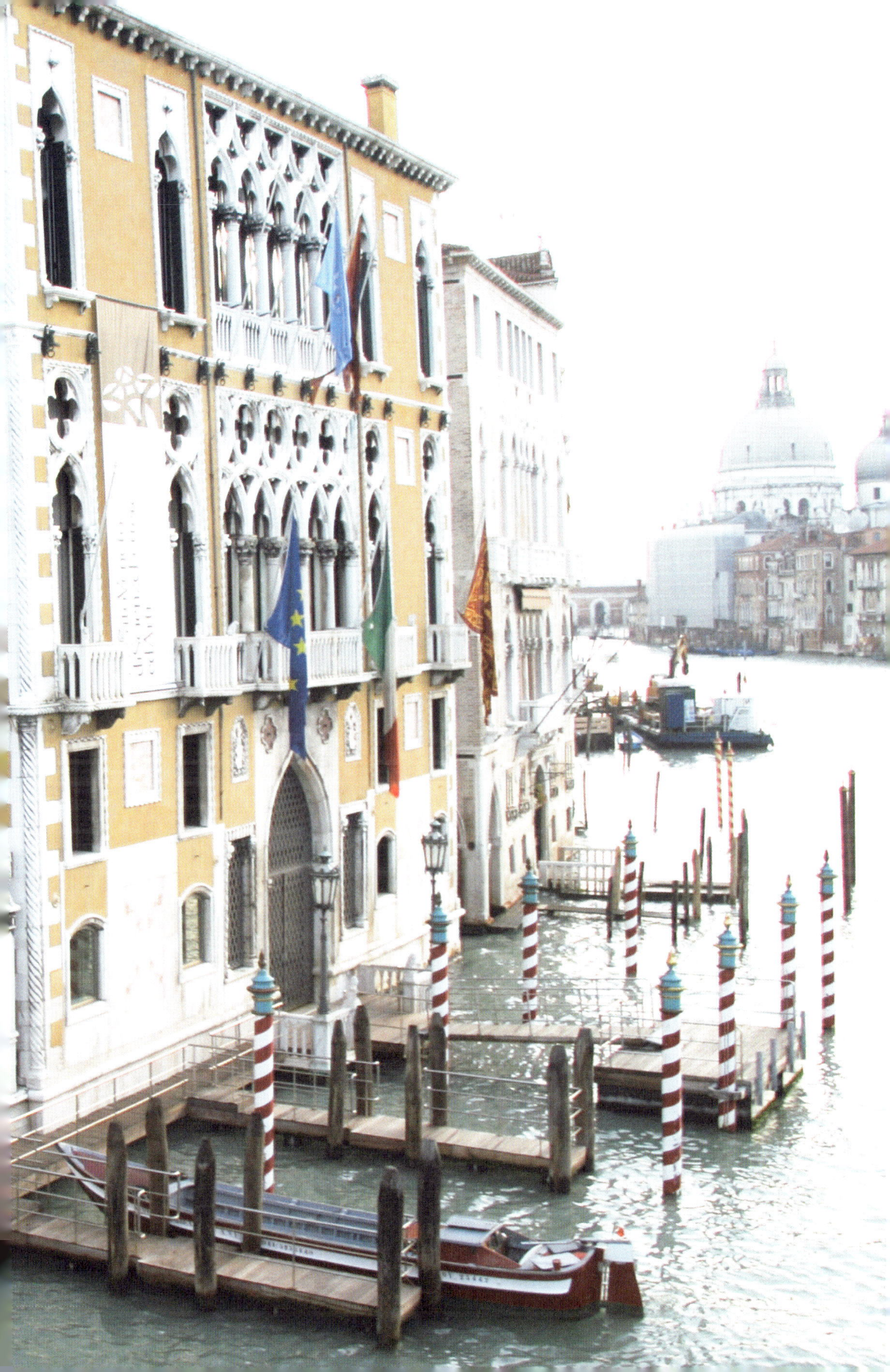

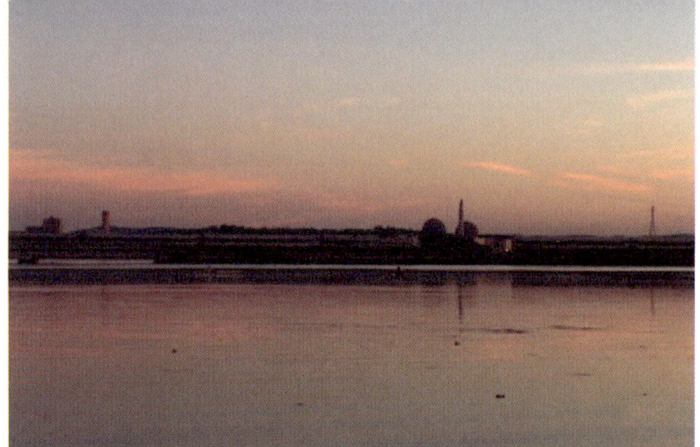

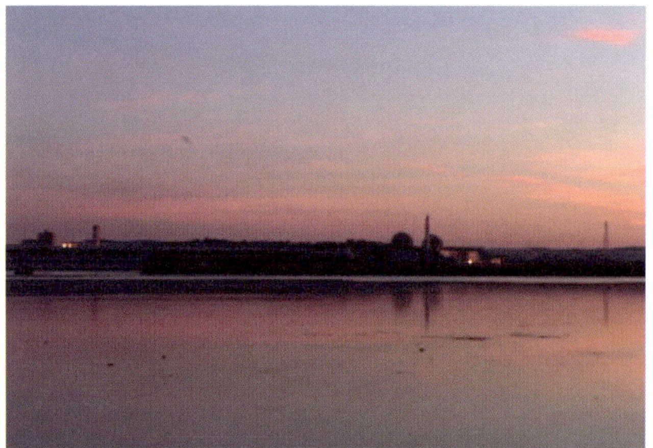

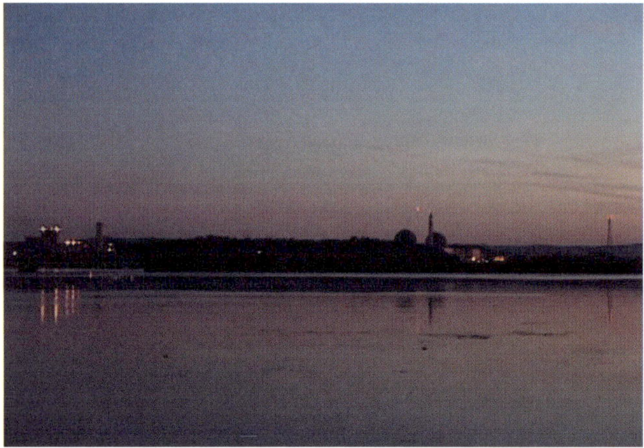

Alan Michelson (Mohawk, b. 1953), three stills from *Twilight, Indian Point*, 2003. Digital video, 31 min., 121.9 x 160 cm. © Alan Michelson.

James Luna (Luiseño, b. 1950), performance for *Emendatio*, 2005 Venice Biennale. Photo by Katherine Fogden. © NMAI.

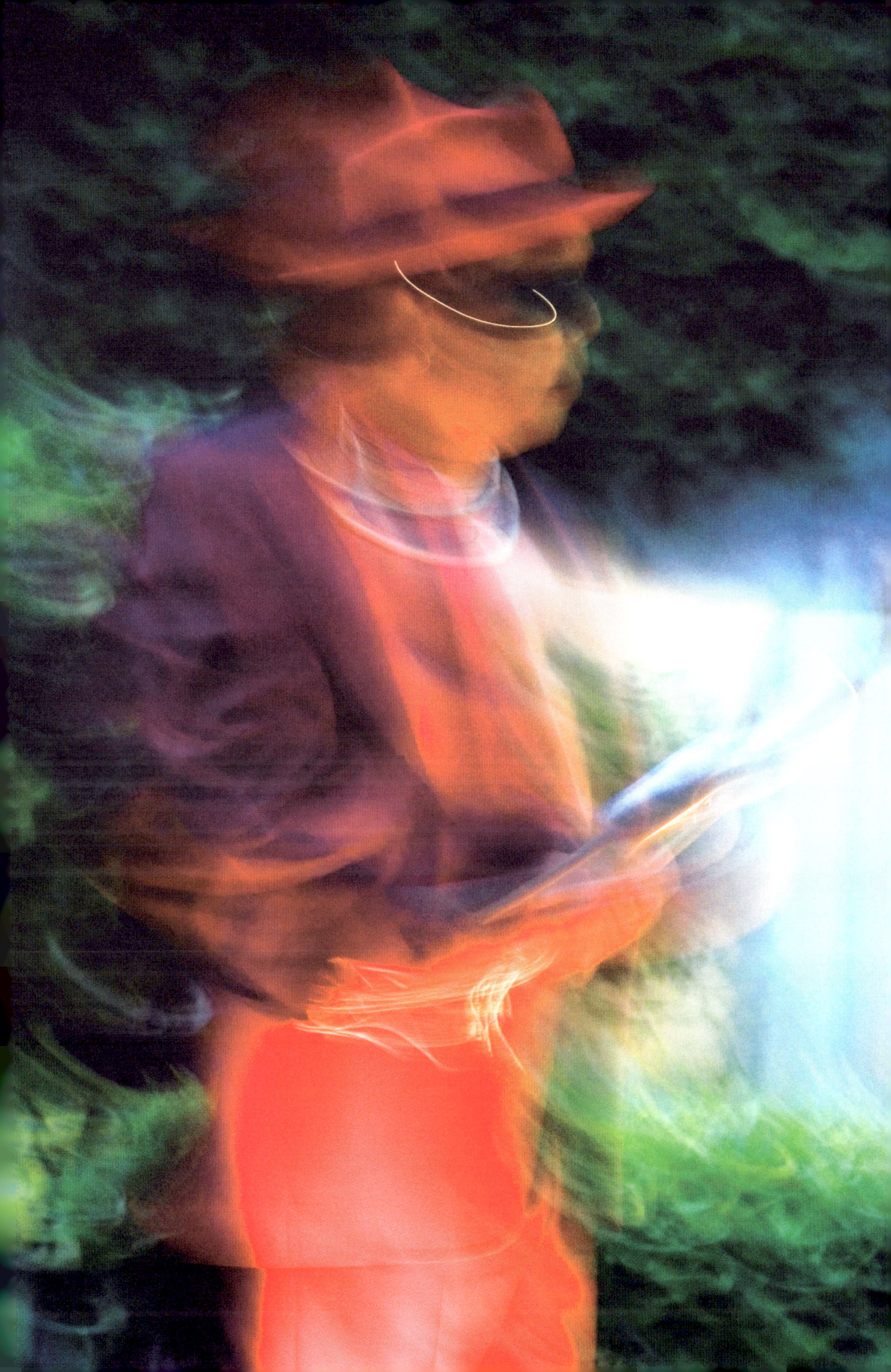

At the Table, in the Big Tent

There is a dialectic going on in the discussion contained in this book, whose contributors' styles and approaches range from personal passion to densely argued cultural politics, and everything in between. The dialectic synthesizes old (world) and new (world) into real (world). I was continually taken with the intellectual ferocity and daring that these writers bring to their collective examination of the state of contemporary art and the role of Native artists within the global cultural community. These artists, curators, scholars—from many nations and states of mind—have kicked the tires and looked under the hood of the old apparatus of Western-dominated art, and they are not buying it. In fact, they are collaborating—conspiring, maybe—to create whole new ways of getting around, of transporting and transforming. If you want a close-up and tangible feel for what such contemporary buzz-words as "globalization" can mean for flesh-and-blood people on the front lines of a cultural transformation, read on. This book will provide its readers with new strategies to frame the ways non-Western cultures are regarded in the global art world.

As director of the National Museum of the American Indian, I have long believed that the museum must play a leading role in bringing to light the neglected work of our many extraordinary Native

American artists. I also believe that the museum can be a force for the recognition of indigenous artists worldwide. In December of 2005, with these priorities in mind, we sponsored a symposium in Venice called *Vision, Space, Desire: Global Perspectives and Cultural Hybridity* to open up an international conversation, on a nexus of issues and concerns, that many of us feel will help define the future of aesthetic expression for indigenous artists. This book grew out of that symposium, which itself followed our sponsorship of the remarkable performance artist James Luna, a member of the La Jolla Band of Mission (Luiseño) Indians, who created a provocative work called *Emendatio* for the Venice Biennale in 2005.

When noted Mohawk artist Alan Michelson wryly remarks in these pages that "the contemporary art world relies upon a global radar system apparently unable to detect Native artists…," I want him to know that the museum will do what it can to get us up there on the screen. In fact, for years now, the National Museum of the American Indian has mounted exhibitions of contemporary Native art, published a number of books on the subject, and brought to the museum—in both Washington, D.C., and New York—not only visual artists, but leading creative writers, musicians and composers, and others. I can promise you that those efforts will continue and increase.

We thank former colleague Gerald McMaster (Plains Cree and member of the Siksika Nation) for chairing the *Vision, Space, Desire* symposium. The distinguished participants in the symposium, some of whom contributed the fine essays found in the pages of this book, also deserve our thanks. We are indebted to project manager Patsy Phillips (Cherokee) for her continued dedication to the furtherance of Native American contemporary art and her skillful guidance of this complex endeavor. Thanks are owed to Nicole Oxendine Poersch (Lumbee) and Ceni Myles (Navajo/Mohegan), and to Tamara Andruszkiewicz in Venice, for their effective work on the organization and logistics of the

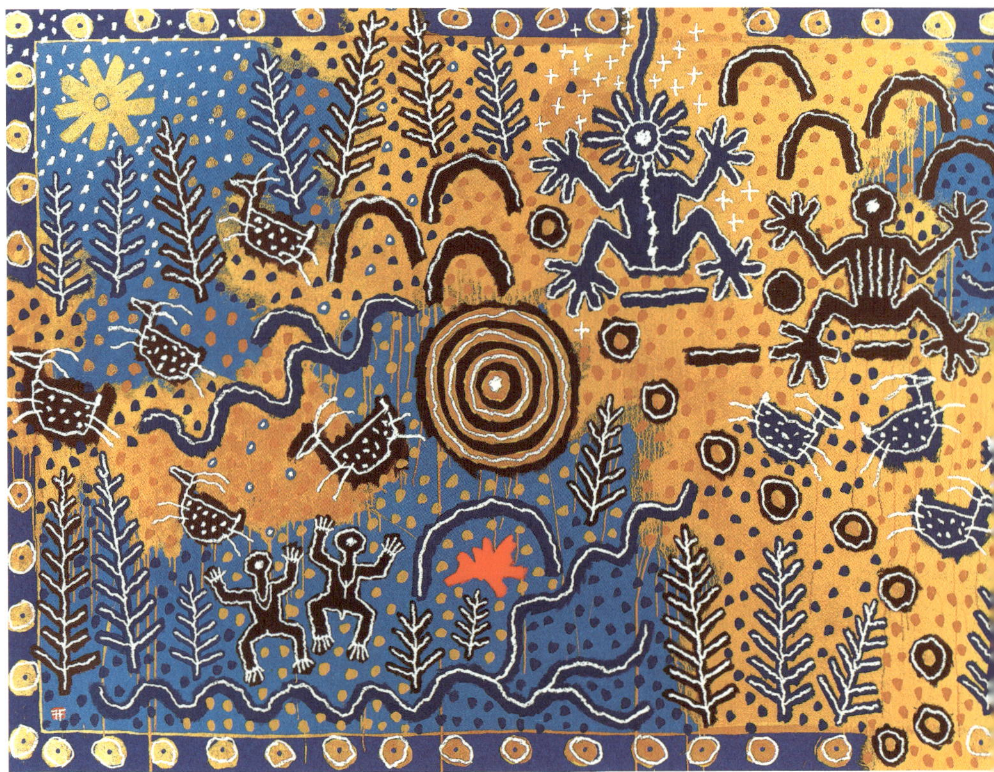

symposium. This book could not have been produced without the commitment of the museum's office of publications, especially head of publications Terence Winch, editor Elizabeth Kennedy Gische, and designer Steve Bell. We are grateful to the Ford Foundation and other friends of the National Museum of the American Indian, whose generous funding made this project possible.

—W. Richard West, Jr.
(Southern Cheyenne and member of the Cheyenne and Arapaho Tribes of Oklahoma)
Founding Director, National Museum of the American Indian

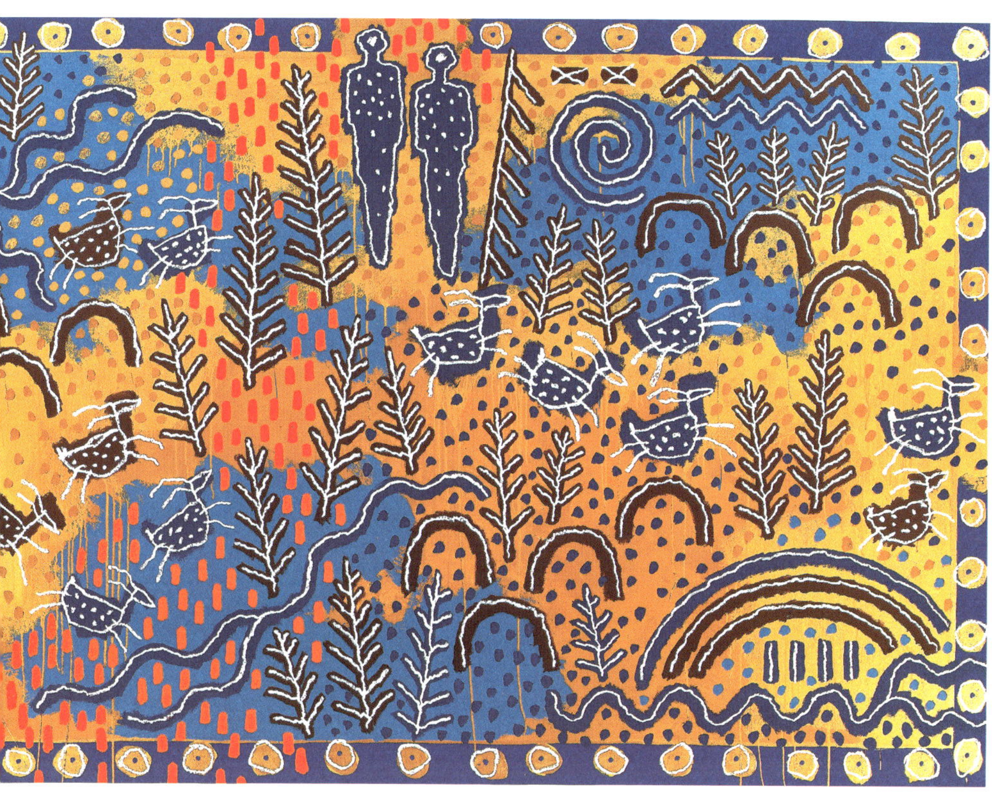

Harry Fonseca (Nisenan Maidu/Hawaiian/Portuguese, b. 1946), *Creation 2001*, 2000. Acrylic on canvas, 203 x 542 cm. Collection of the National Museum of the American Indian (26/5007). Photo by Ernest Amoroso. © NMAI.

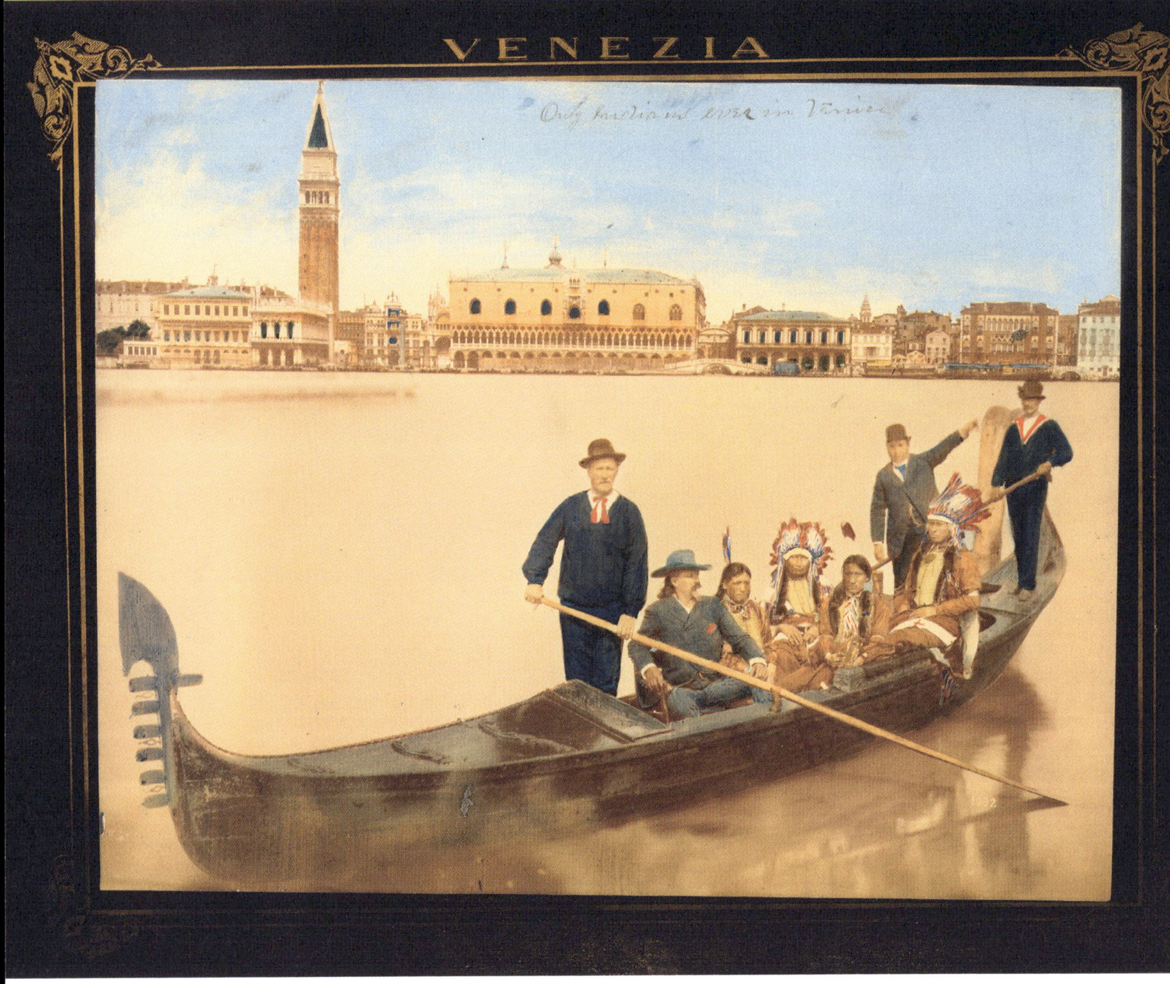

"Only Indians Ever in Venice." Hand-colored photograph, ca. 1890. Photo by Paolo Salviati. © Buffalo Bill Historical Center, Cody, Wyoming; P.69.822.

GERALD McMASTER

New Art/New Contexts

As the Canadian Commissioner to the 1995 Venice Biennale, I curated an exhibition on the work of contemporary Métis artist Edward Poitras. Among the images in the show's catalogue is an 1890 photograph of William F. "Buffalo Bill" Cody and his entourage of Native Americans afloat in a Venetian gondola. Handwritten across the top of the photograph are the words, "Only Indians ever in Venice." This group of Lakota (Sioux) had come to Italy with Cody to perform in the nearby city of Verona. An excursion to Venice culminated with the flamboyant Cody parading around the city with the Indians.

I chose the image for its evocation of the historical weight of otherness, exoticism, and invisibility—issues that have preoccupied Native American art critics while stirring little concern within an international art context. Back in Venice a decade later, I find that the photograph of Buffalo Bill and his Plains Indian companions on the Grand Canal provides a fruitful point of departure for our discussion of global connections and cultural hybridities.

Venice 2005

The Smithsonian's National Museum of the American Indian (NMAI) opened the doors of its museum on the National Mall in Washington, D.C., to the public on September 21, 2004, the autumnal equinox. Dedicated exclusively to the art and culture of the indigenous people of the Western Hemisphere, the museum joined NMAI's George Gustav Heye Center in New York City, open since 1994, in presenting exhibitions and programs in the indigenous voice. The Heye Center regularly features the works of contemporary Native artists, and NMAI's museum on the Mall showcased the paintings, drawings, and sculpture of two preeminent Native American modernists, Allan Houser (Warm Springs Chiricahua Apache, 1914–1994) and George Morrison (Grand Portage Band of Chippewa, 1919–2000), in one of its inaugural exhibitions.

As part of its commitment to supporting contemporary art beyond these two venues, the museum sponsored celebrated performance artist James Luna (Luiseño) at the 2005 Venice Biennale in *Emendatio*, an exhibit and performance at the Fondazione Querini Stampalia, publishing a unique book to commemorate the project. Canada sent its premier performance artist Rebecca Belmore (Anishinabe). The simultaneous appearance of these two highly regarded Native performance artists at one of the world's most prestigious art exhibitions raises important questions. How is this significant moment to be celebrated? Is it an occasion to question and examine the diverse artistic practices flourishing in regions outside of the West? International art shows, such as the Venice, São Paulo, or Istanbul exhibitions, provide people in the arts with many opportunities to appraise new currents and to assess their location in relation to the larger world. With this in mind, the organizers of this project felt a need for debate in an expansive critical context. We seized the moment by inviting artists, curators, museum directors, academics, and critics from various parts of the world to join us for a symposium in Venice to examine several key issues and ideas. That symposium, *Vision, Space, Desire: Global Perspectives and Cultural Hybridity,* provided the basis for this book.

Conditions

A look at some of the most common issues regarding Native American contemporary art—authenticity, marketing Indian art, trademarks, stereotypes/mascots, appropriation/copyright—reveals how well-trodden the discourse has become. While these are important issues, we hope to add a fresh perspective to the discussion in this book of the realities and complexity of the contemporary art world. First, I would like to delineate a number of conditions that still affect the work of Native contemporary artists and curators—even as they look outward for inspiration and partake in national and international exhibitions.

The First Condition: The Discourse of the Past

Institutionally and culturally, through most of the twentieth century, indigenous people have been represented largely through the discursive space and authority of Western museums of anthropology. Native artists have been ambivalent about this relationship. Largely limited to exhibiting their work in these institutional spaces until as late as the 1980s, Native contemporary artists realized the art world in general was rapidly changing, and they became the vanguard. They began finding new audiences for their work and patrons who were receptive to their new expressions; they also began critiquing the practice of museums. In his now famous *The Artifact Piece* (1987), James Luna staged a critique that struck at the very heart of the anthropological museum, startling the complacent visitor. As in the traditional Sundance rituals of the Lakota and other Plains tribes, Luna made a bodily sacrifice. In some ways, this performance was akin to works by American performance artist Chris Burden, whose outrageous performances include one in which he crucified himself to the back of a Volkswagen. In Burden's and some other performance artists' works, it seemed the threshold of physical pain was the objective; for Luna, it was the emotional pain of hundreds of years of injustice and mistreatment of indigenous people. Although it was a performance piece, Luna's landmark work was not presented to an art audience; his initial audience consisted of everyday visitors to the

Museum of Man, an anthropological museum in San Diego, California.

The Artifact Piece has risen to an iconic level. Luna's minimal, brilliant, and emotional performance created an intellectual shift away from the condition in which Native people were objectified and spoken for or treated in third-person perspective. Native people now said: "We are here. We have survived, and we are contributing." We asserted our right to be treated on an equal basis as first persons or subjects. How did Luna's performance piece do this? Quite simply, he sat up, stepped out of the vitrine he had been lying in, and walked—much to the surprise and ultimate intellectual awakening of those who happened to be standing nearby, absentmindedly gazing at an ostensibly inanimate Indian body.

The Second Condition: The Discourse of Gatekeeping

The Indian Arts and Crafts Act of 1990 (P.L. 101-644) prohibits misrepresentation in marketing Indian art and craft products within the United States. The legislation states that only members of Indian tribes recognized by federal or state governments can legally exhibit or advertise themselves as Indian artists. Its original intent was to protect the traditional arts—such as jewelry, pottery, baskets, and so on—from being copied by non-Indians and falsely sold as "Indian art." Individuals and families have long owned tribal rights to designs and other intellectual property, but since these rights had not been respected for most of the twentieth century, U.S. law was needed to curb wanton appropriation. The Indian Arts and Crafts Board of the U.S. Department of the Interior declares: "All products must be marketed truthfully regarding the Indian heritage and tribal affiliation of the producers, so as not to mislead the consumer."

Challenges arose when a number of artists previously thought of as Native American could not prove their authenticity or membership in a tribe recognized by the government. Native individuals who had been adopted and thus lost connection with their tribes were particularly hard hit. The Indian Arts and Crafts Act, however, does not apply to work by Canadian or Latin American indigenous artists. The unintended consequences of this law and its effect on contemporary art practice have given rise to a number of questions regarding the relevance of this condition within the contemporary art world. The internationally recognized American artist Jimmie Durham, a self-identified Cherokee, is among the artists who encountered political storms over this issue. Rather than endure legal challenges, Durham has gone into exile and moved on; yet many others critique the law's efficacy.

The Third Condition: The Discourse of Postcolonialism

Living in a postcolonial, postmodern world is a confounding condition. Although the postcolonial movement is largely a phenomenon of the past half-century, it has been argued that everyone has been colonized at some time or other. Many continue to be culturally and economically subordinated to rich industrial nations. Nonetheless, diverse areas and cultures in Africa, Asia, and elsewhere have gained independence from European countries and asserted their sovereignty. In contrast, indigenous cultures in the Americas and Australia remain in neocolonial situations. The transmigration of various peoples and cultures across the world—some managing to maintain certain traditions and practices, others blending with their adopted countries—further complicates the situation. Postmodernism has been a feature of Western, postindustrial cultures since the late twentieth century. The postcolonial and postmodern movements both examine ideas of authority or "control" in different settings.

New ideas and approaches have transformed contemporary artistic and curatorial practices. Consider, for example, the major themes of postcolonial discourse in relation to criticism: historiography and the practice of art; the process of cultural globalization now taking place around a multiplicity of centers; or the mobility, flexibility, and nomadism of contemporary life, which have become metaphors for today's condition. On an increasingly complex and connected globe, the art world is expanding far beyond the Western trajectory. The old patterns of exclusion have reversed, bringing new voices into the mainstream.

The Fourth Condition: The Discourse of Center/Periphery

(Native) contemporary artists live and practice in highly contested spaces that collide and mix and are continually subject to negotiation. These artists move in and among many different kinds of environments—traditional and contemporary, Native and non-Native peoples, rural and urban places, the core and margins of society—and make art for many reasons, including as a means of persistence and identity. In the game of perception, artists constantly search for a periphery, knowing that moving just beyond it will bring out the trickster in them, either as a form of inspiration, a radical expression, or a new practice. Though centers and peripheries are imaginary, constructed, loose, mobile, and ever-changing, they help us understand the nature of contemporary artistic practice.

Some artists perceive the centers of production (the markets) as being out of their reach in the larger cities. In reaction, they have become consciously aware of "center" as an idea and realize how its perception can be influenced. Shifting our perspective, they help us to understand that centers include culture, language, and family, among other loci. Encompassing rural and urban, reservations and reserves, these newly claimed centers of reference are an unending source of inspiration.

The Symposium

To mark the conclusion of a Biennale that included two prominent Native artists, we invited many of our friends and colleagues from various countries to come to Venice to share new ideas in theory and research. We held the *Vision, Space, Desire* symposium at the Istituto Veneto di Scienze, Lettere ed Arti in the Palazzo Cavalli Franchetti on December 13, 2005. The gathering was also timed to build upon the panels, lectures, and discussions of the international symposium *Where Art Worlds Meet: Multiple Modernities and the Global Salon*, which was organized by Robert Storr, recently named as director of the 2007 Venice Biennale's 52nd International Art Exhibition, and took place at the Istituto Veneto di Scienze, Lettere ed Arti from December 9 through 12.

Vision, Space, Desire explored indigenous artistic and curatorial practices in relation to various perspectival and theoretical debates ongoing throughout the contemporary art world. The symposium promoted a lively international dialogue and exchange of ideas among Native and non-Native museum directors and curators, artists, critics, and scholars and opened new possibilities in contemporary art practice and engagement. Topics included institutional and alternative spaces of practice; the politics of curatorial practice; globalization, diaspora and indigeneity; and the relevance of postmodern and postcolonial theories in reading Native contemporary art.

Our aim is to construct a picture of the current situation and its inherent dynamics, and identify ways to increase the profile of key issues in the minds of those pivotal to contemporary art world discourse. The symposium provided a forum for contributors to voice new ideas and explore innovative interdisciplinary frameworks. The majority of participants are not Native people, or even non-Indians who have been identified with indigenous art practices; we wished to avoid the impression that the symposium was an expected presentation of "our issues" to those who have "done wrong" and ignored Indian art. We wanted this symposium to produce unexpected insights and map new directions for the future.

Vision, Space, Desire

I would like to provide a few insights about our title. "Vision" is about looking back, looking sideways, and looking forward. Looking back concerns where we have come from and what gives each of us our identity; looking sideways tells us what is happening elsewhere by revealing other discourses, issues, ideas, and strategies; and looking forward is about moving into the future together, sharing ideas and issues, and exchanging strategies. "Space" is not only about looking at the local and global but also the relations between the two—how we are influenced by local discourses and how we translate them to larger audiences and platforms. "Desire" refers to our wish to expand our frames of reference as we move toward new forms and terms of participation in the rapidly evolving international contemporary art world.

Sessions and Questions

The symposium was organized into two large sessions; "New Contact Zones" took place in the morning, followed by "Performing Cultural Hybridity" in the afternoon. We formulated and posed to panelists certain core questions that addressed Native contemporary artistic and curatorial issues in relation to other (Western and Eastern European, African, and Latin American) theoretical discussions and experiences. Questions for the first session included:

- What is the international art world's perception of art done outside either the West or the mainstream, such as Native American contemporary art?

- Does your institution present or include contemporary Native art? Why or why not?

- How has the postmodern/postcolonial discourse affected institutional frameworks? Has this discourse opened up intellectual and curatorial space?

- Is it a good idea to have a separate institution for non-Western art or non-male art, such as the Musée du Quai Branly in Paris or National Museum of Women in the Arts in Washington, D.C.? How are non-Western institutions creating relations with mainstream institutions?

For the afternoon session, "Performing Cultural Hybridity," we posed the following questions:

- Is the work done by Native American contemporary artists still being reduced to ethnic or racial lines?

- Is the Western or mainstream art institution still a site of struggle for non-Western artists?

- Why is it that the Native American contemporary artist can belong neither to the West nor to modernity?

- Is there a trend toward inclusion of non-Western artists in major mainstream contemporary art exhibitions?

- What are the new productive sites of practice?

As part of this landmark project, we invited a number of special guest curators and artists who had attended the *Vision, Space, Desire* symposium but were not presenters at the formal sessions to contribute their individual reflections about the symposium to this book. These informal, thought-provoking pieces are included under the rubric "Personal Reflections" in the third section of the volume.

The Presentations

Vision, Space, Desire finished with a performance by James Luna, during which he made reference to the "false face" of recognition, which I took to mean that his elevated status during and after the Biennale resulted in few telephone calls from curators. Ironically, his use of the term "false face" hit directly at the core of our motive for the symposium.

The symposium was an attempt to bring together a disparate group of professionals in a moment where difference was temporarily suspended and similarities shared. The gathering confirmed our expectation that each participant would offer new perspectives; it also revealed that much work remains to be done, that received or emerging discourses still need to be pushed, prodded, and challenged. The juxtaposition with *Where Art Worlds Meet* produced unexpected yet positive results, as the symposium participants made numerous and illuminating references to the Storr conference.

Indeed, some of our participants were included in the Storr conference, such as art critic/scholar Jean Fisher, a tireless advocate of contemporary artists who practice outside the mainstream. We knew that her articulate voice and powerful analysis would be critical to our success. We were not disappointed by her paper " 'New Contact Zones': A Reflection."

Next, art historian/curator/editor Salah Hassan spoke about *Authentic/Ex-Centric: Africa in and out of Africa*, an exhibition he co-curated with Olu Oguibe as part of the 49th Venice Biennale. He addressed the difficulty involved in changing the minds of Biennale officials, and noted that only one African country, Egypt, has maintained a national pavilion. This situation will be transformed in the 2007 Biennale, which will include an African Pavilion offering an informed and distinctive perspective on current work being made on the African continent, and, at the discretion of the curators, in the African diaspora. Salah also said: "If you don't exhibit, you don't exist." He could have added, "If you don't publish, you don't exist," because *Nka: Journal of Contemporary African Art,* of which he is an editor, has played a strategic role in positioning African art in the international arena.

Artist and scholar Jolene Rickard (Tuscarora) presented a paper in which she asks a number of profound questions that could form the basis for a whole other symposium. Referencing the invisibility about which Salah spoke and the current intense interest in China, for example, she asks: "If 'big' works for the Chinese, why doesn't small work for us?" Jolene concludes by saying that *Vision, Space, Desire* was our survivance against erasure in which we offer up our presence.

Australian artist and curator Brenda Croft's humorous yet direct pronouncement that Aboriginal people were underrepresented in exhibitions but overrepresented in jails (or in ethnographic museums as objects) hit some nerves. Explaining that she is an Aboriginal woman from the Gurindji/Mutpurra nations in the Northern Territory of Australia, she says, "I became a curator by default"; the necessity of such a move for self-representation has also been experienced by indigenous people in the Western Hemisphere. Noting that some artists in her country have repudiated their Aboriginality in favor of internationalism, Brenda asked: "Why can't we have both?"

Brazilian curator Ivo Mesquita brought a Brazilian and Latin American perspective to the issues we addressed and presented some points about strategic planning to include contemporary Native artistic productions and practices into an evermore interdependent and globalized circuit. In response to the question of whether or not to have separate museums for non-Western art, Ivo cautions: "The problem arises when contemporary artists turn these museums into ideological trenches, instead of seeking new spaces for confrontation, shock, or friction. Being in the world, subjected to the turbulences of life, seems to me the necessary condition of being an artist as well as a curator."

Anthropologist Nancy Marie Mithlo (Chiricahua Apache) is the director of the arts collective Indigenous Arts Action Alliance (IA3), which has brought Native contemporary artists to the Venice Biennale since 1999. She writes about strategies of taking artists outside local "Indian markets" into international spaces of practice to find new and different points of reference.

A short "Question, Answer, and Statement" period allowed Harry Fonseca (Nisenan Maidu/Hawaiian/Portuguese) to say that group shows must be replaced by exhibitions on individual artists. Edgar Heap of Birds (Cheyenne/Arapaho) commented that Native artists have become insular by seeing themselves as different and therefore special. Another asserted that we live in—to use Robert Hughes's phrase— "a culture of complaint" when we should be taking the initiative to make change. How to do this? We need to found our own journal, similar to Salah's *Nka: Journal of Contemporary African Art,* instead of waiting for mainstream journals to make a move.

My symposium colleague Paul Chaat Smith (Comanche) recalled Jimmie Durham's statement that "Europe is an Indian project," which I take to mean that the long-standing relationship between Europeans and Native Americans continues and, furthermore, that indigenous artists need to keep on making their presence known here and around the world. If post-colonialism is but a fantasy for Native Americans, then it requires other strategies; perhaps *Vision, Space, Desire,* as our effort to contribute in the international dialogue, is such a project.

Curator Lee-Ann Martin (Mohawk) moderated the afternoon session, "Performing Cultural Hybridity." Her "performance and artistic mobility" strategy referenced Ronald Wright's view of the "new world order," a condition where half the world takes away from the other half. No doubt she would agree that the economically richer half still has a lot to learn from the other.

Sylvie Fortin, editor-in-chief of *Art Papers,* provided insight into how large international exhibitions such as biennales often use the multicultural "other" as an interchangeable part processed through a system of expectations that she describes as a kind of "yellow pages" approach. She then offers propositions for developing sustainable practices through fostering research and producing particular spaces of opportunity. Institutions such as the National Museum of the American Indian need to invest in such programmatic areas. Venice is not enough for Native contemporary artists; they need to proceed in multiple directions to build connections with non-Native institutions inside and outside the United States.

Art museum director and curator Paulo Herkenhoff's resoluteness about artists as agents of change was especially poignant. His reference point was his country of Brazil, where the indigenous and the countless poor are routinely relegated to the margins of society, a place of invisibility he calls the "Third Bank." For him it is a void, "where no air is available for the voice to travel," and people are considered worthless. He speaks of the West as the "Bank of Nothing" in relation to indigenous peoples and the mentally ill, using Brazilian artist Cildo Meireles's enigmatic work *Zero Cruzeiro* (1974–78) to illustrate his paper.

Toronto artist/curator Robert Houle (First Nations Saulteaux) spoke of both non- and misrecognition as damaging ways of framing "otherness" for Native peoples and artists upon whom a national identity in which we are considered foreign is superimposed. Native artists, however, are working strategically to create their own spaces of identity within Western countries such as Canada and the United States.

Vasif Kortun, director of Platform Garanti Contemporary Art Center in Istanbul, told a story of his journey to Germany in the late 1980s, armed with slides, where he was seeking opportunities for Turkish artists. Instead, he met only with frustration. Upon returning home, he determined to start new projects that would create a favorable condition for local artists. A process that began fifteen years ago continues today. In the intervening time, he has noticed how Turkish artists are now looking for regional exchanges of ideas that he describes as "horizontal conversations." And they are not looking to New York or other large Western cities, but to spaces such as Zagreb or Cairo.

New Zealand curator Megan Tamati-Quennell (Te Atiäwä/Ngäi Tahu/Käti Mamoe) spoke about a unique brand of cultural hybridity. Mäori people construct *whakapapa* (the Maori "wh" is pronounced as "f," making it "faka-papa"), which entails a genealogical recitation that moves forward from the past. After New Zealand Europeans arrived, for example, this Māori knowledge system and frame of reference was expanded to incorporate them. Such strategies of inclusion—of the expansion of customary cultural concepts—performed by Māori artists, she says, constitute an attempt to create one's own space and then project it out onto the world.

Where Art Worlds Meet

I would be remiss without a reflection on Robert Storr's conference, in which speaker after speaker eloquently addressed issues and ideas surrounding the notion of the "biennale." At present, there are at least 110 biennales world-wide, and counting. Venice, running since 1895, and São Paulo, begun in 1951, stand out from the group. Because biennales were often tied to nationalism, Storr reports, the good ones are conscious of their localities. The purpose is not to sell modernity to the public but rather to engage them in such a way as to suggest they were interlocutors. The biennale's role is to put the public in contact with the art of its time. Storr spoke about art fairs, another phenomenon of today's commercially driven art world, and asks: How can institutions participate in these kaleidoscopic events? He suggests that institutions loan or rent out objects from their collections.

A few highlights from the conference: Swiss economist Bruno Frey observed that art institutions today are so worried about the numbers game that they forget to do what they do best, which is to focus on the artistic value they provide to the public. He says not to concentrate on what he calls "pseudo-economics," but on the arts! Ackbar Abbas spoke about issues in China today, noting that China wants to change its identity without losing its past; so, for example, because there is nostalgia for the Cultural Revolution, some restaurants still sell "Cultural Revolution food" that is quite bad—it is better to put up with bad food than the uncertainties of the future. He says suspending value doesn't mean that one is giving it up; rather, that there are no models to follow, so one has to create new ones. Ann Deathridge complained that administrators do not understand cultural and social capital. She also argues that "ethnicity" is a dangerous platform for artists to use as it can become their cultural albatross. Lynne Cooke maintains that there is no installation art; instead there are installation practices that grew out of artists responding as a form of "specularization" to various activities.

Jean-Hubert Martin argues that dialogue with non-Western cultures was always from the perspective of a Western scale of values, and in postcolonial times, these values need to be reassessed. He says minority artists have different issues, such as fighting for their rights, which are beyond the interest of the contemporary art world; these artists are dealt with as exotics. Martin criticized the "universal language of art" as a kind of Western Esperanto where the West is the point of reference that ignores others. Vasif Kortun spoke about the 2005 Istanbul Biennial. The curators viewed the city of Istanbul, an old city that is also contemporary, as a space with many possibilities; they arranged for artists to spend three weeks to six months in the city to come up with a work that worked with, around, and through the city. The Cuban art critic Gerardo Mosquera spoke about the first Havana Biennial, which focused on Latin American and Third World artists. Using the motto "Revolution with Fun," artists were encouraged to create their own space and project it onto the world. The Havana Biennial did not lose its local character to become engrossed in the "big-show syndrome"; the curators used the idea of the "Bar" as a synecdoche for spaces of encounters and a means to create accessible spaces. Finally, Wu Hung spoke about the Beijing Biennale and the fact that contemporary Chinese art has transcended local space and is now in a global space. How can a biennale such as Beijing's, he asks, retain its non-Western identity through the idea of "flattening," of connecting with the local, instead of the other way around?

At the end of the conference, Storr said the Venice Biennale is the "mother of all biennales," one that is based on the old world order. In the twenty-first century, we have a very different picture. In this context, what is the opportunity or possibility of a "new world order" in which emerging nations and indigenous nations-within-nations have a voice? Perhaps the dialogue has begun with the juxtaposition of Storr's conference with the National Museum of the American Indian's symposium.

Conclusion

When Native people attack James Luna for taking on in his art the problems of alcoholism, poverty, and violence in Native communities, he explains that he is not just criticizing a condition, he is in the condition. So it is with the National Museum of the American Indian. We are at the center of all the contradictions that shape how Native art is produced, collected, sold and bought, displayed, and received. *Vision, Space, Desire* signals our interest in beginning a wide-ranging discussion among peers about these issues, recognizing that none of us have the answers but rather that we are engaged in a mutual search for understanding.

Finally, we would like to thank W. Richard West, Jr. (Southern Cheyenne), founding director of the National Museum of the American Indian, for his unwavering and visionary commitment to Native contemporary art, of which his steadfast support for the *Vision, Space, Desire* symposium and book is but one instance.

Gerald McMaster (Plains Cree and member of the Siksika Nation) is curator of Canadian art at the Art Gallery of Ontario. Recipient of Canada's 2005 National Aboriginal Achievement Award, McMaster worked with the Smithsonian's National Museum of the American Indian from 2000 to 2005, where he was deputy assistant director for cultural resources and later responsible for the design and content of three permanent exhibitions.

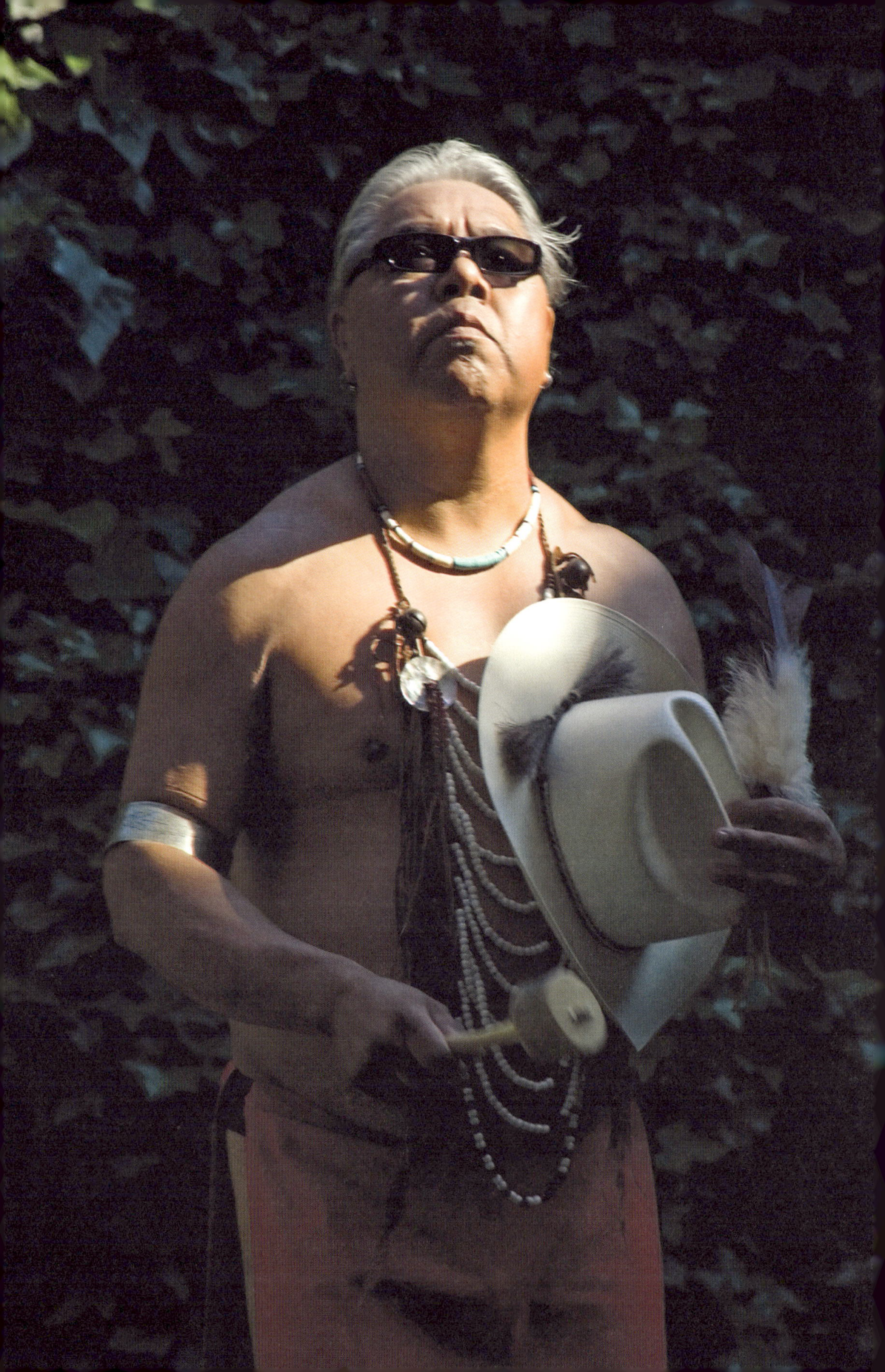

PAUL CHAAT SMITH

DELTA ONE FIFTY

Welcome to *Vision, Space, Desire: Global Perspectives and Cultural Hybridity.* My name is Paul Chaat Smith, I'm Comanche, I live in Washington, D.C., and am an associate curator at the Smithsonian's National Museum of the American Indian (NMAI). Gerald McMaster (Plains Cree and member of the Siksika Nation) is the chair of the symposium, and so he bears most of the responsibility for this event, but I'm also implicated because I am the second most responsible person. Complaints should go to him, compliments to me.

The title of my presentation is "Delta One Fifty" and it's about airplanes, genocide, and rainbows.

Which I'll get to right away, after bringing everyone up to date on recent developments. As you know, the 51st International Art Exhibition of the Venice Biennale featured James Luna (Luiseño) at the Fondazione Querini Stampalia, and Rebecca Belmore (Anishinabe) at the Canadian Pavilion. The two shows were smash hits and made them both rich and famous. How rich, you ask. Well, in the last few months, Luna bought Jay-Z's old place in Malibu, the Rock and Roll Hall of Fame and Museum in Cleveland, and a pair of teal blue Lamborghinis. Interestingly enough, although he could easily have resigned his position as academic counselor at Palomar College, the Jesus of Cool still shows up for work just like before, except now he arrives by helicopter.

James Luna (Luiseño, b. 1950), performance for *Emendatio*, 2005 Venice Biennale. Photo by Katherine Fogden. © NMAI.

Rebecca bought Pier D of the Vancouver International Airport. She's transformed Gates 49 through 56 into a rehearsal space for current projects, like turning passengers boarding flights to Calgary into performative readymades. It's a temporary arrangement, just until Doug Cardinal finishes building that castle up on Whistler Mountain. None of us were especially surprised that our most regal artist will soon be living in a castle. Actually, some of us thought she already lived in one . . . "so she's getting a bigger castle or what?" We were shocked, however, to hear last week that the Cardinal project is on time and under budget. Truman Lowe (Ho-Chunk), who curated the Luna thing with me, bought a nice cottage on Lake Monona, and I've been busy with my new column for *Artforum*, plus last week I signed a six-figure contract for a book I'm writing on Damien Hirst.

So it's pretty funny to think about how only a year ago lots of people at the museum thought the whole Venice deal was a ridiculous boondoggle. Ha, look who's laughing now [interrupted by NMAI staff person who hands PCS a note]. Okay, sorry, Nicole informs me that nothing of what I just said was actually true. I'm also supposed to apologize for all the inside jokes, which will be explained when we publish the proceedings. Hey, I was just kidding! We didn't really make out like bandits! If you want to buy their work or book them for an exhibition, Rebecca and James would love to hear from you. And yo, Tim Griffin, seriously, call me, let's talk. . . .

Life after Venice is not radically different than before Venice, or even liberally different. It's much the same, actually. But how did we get here, and why are we back?

Indians in Venice

A very brief history of Indians in Venice begins in recent times with the selection of Gerald McMaster as Commissioner for the Canadian Pavilion for the 1995 Venice Biennale, and Gerald's selection of Métis artist Edward Poitras. That made Edward a household name in the houses of art-loving sophisticates in Canada, and a hero to many Indians, mostly also in Canada. But lots of us heard about this, though we didn't know too much about the Venice Biennale. Also, and not particularly connected to the Poitras show,

Jimmie Durham has been a regular at the Arsenale. And also, not particularly connected either, a group of artists and activists based in Santa Fe staged their own exhibitions at the Biennale in 1999, 2001, and 2003. Nancy Marie Mithlo (Chiricahua Apache) spoke about that. In 2003, my institution sponsored a reception with them to host Mohawk artist Shelley Niro. Everybody had a great time, which led the National Museum of the American Indian to decide we should come back, and we launched a project to try to win the United States Pavilion in 2005. We decided that if we were not selected, we would go to the Biennale anyway as a collateral project. We never got a chance to compete for the U.S. Pavilion, and partnered with the Fondazione Querini Stampalia. It was pure serendipity that Rebecca Belmore, like James a performance and installation artist, was selected to represent Canada. It made us feel like we were on the right track, and we began hyping these interventions as Indian summer in Venice.

My point here is that there was no grand scheme or anything inevitable about Luna and Belmore in Venice in 2005. I would argue, however, that even if Poitras had never been chosen by Canada ten years ago, if Gerald McMaster had decided to remain a painter instead of becoming an international curator, or if the NMAI didn't have a visionary director who strongly supported contemporary art, Indian artists would still have dreamed about Venice, because artists all over the world dream of Venice. In the larger sense, Indians in Venice were inevitable, because our best artists are really, really good, and like really good artists anywhere, they want to be in the most important shows. Indians were going to be here sooner or later, one way or another, because that's what we do, we go places and do things.

The NMAI is one of the few Indian institutions with the resources to pull off a project of this size. The symposium came about partly because the Ford Foundation was interested in it. So we studied what Salah Hassan did here in 2001 and borrowed liberally from his *Authentic/Ex-Centric* project. We thought about having a symposium in Rome or New York or Berlin or Washington, but when we learned of the Storr symposium and read about its intentions, we decided to see if we could somehow make our discussions connect. This is normally the place where the story turns ugly, the parties are suspicious, intrigues are launched, and it's all a big disaster. Except that didn't happen. Instead, our reception has been respectful and warm, the Biennale has advertised and endorsed *Vision, Space, Desire*, and so here we are. So far, everybody seems to mean what they say.

For me, there are three reasons why we are in Venice. The first two are good ones and important but not super-important. A few months ago, Rosa Martinez, co-curator of the 2005 Biennale, gave an interview about her experience and said one of her main regrets was that she didn't have the time to travel and research art production around the world, so she was limited to looking at artists who had been in other biennales/biennials. James Luna and Rebecca Belmore have been major figures for decades, but neither had been in the major art festivals. They were off the map, now they are on it. The second reason is that the crew that organized *Vision, Space, Desire* believed that the discourse around contemporary Native art was stale and in need of new ideas and new energy. Which is why, instead of a panel of only Indians, we have a panel of Indians and non-Indians, some of whom are not expert on our issues at all. This is quite controversial, since it obviously means we are leaving talented Indian artists and scholars off the agenda and replacing them with people from Turkey and England.

But the third reason is the most important. We have a responsibility to be here. I wish someone else had said it better but no one has, so I will reference once again artist Jimmie Durham. He wrote that Europe is an Indian project. Europe is an Indian project—now, that sounds intriguing, a little mysterious, and goes well with another formula, this one in the public domain of Indian truisms, which is that every place is an Indian place. But what are we really talking about here?

Let me break this down. For a long, long time, not like geologic time or even dinosaur time, but believe me, a really, really long time, half of the world didn't know about the other half. Africa, Asia, and Europe knew of each other, even if much of what they knew was rumor and misinformation. They were pretty sure they constituted the world. The Americas, which weren't the Americas yet, didn't know anything about Europe and Asia and Africa. The people not yet Americans were fairly sure they were the whole

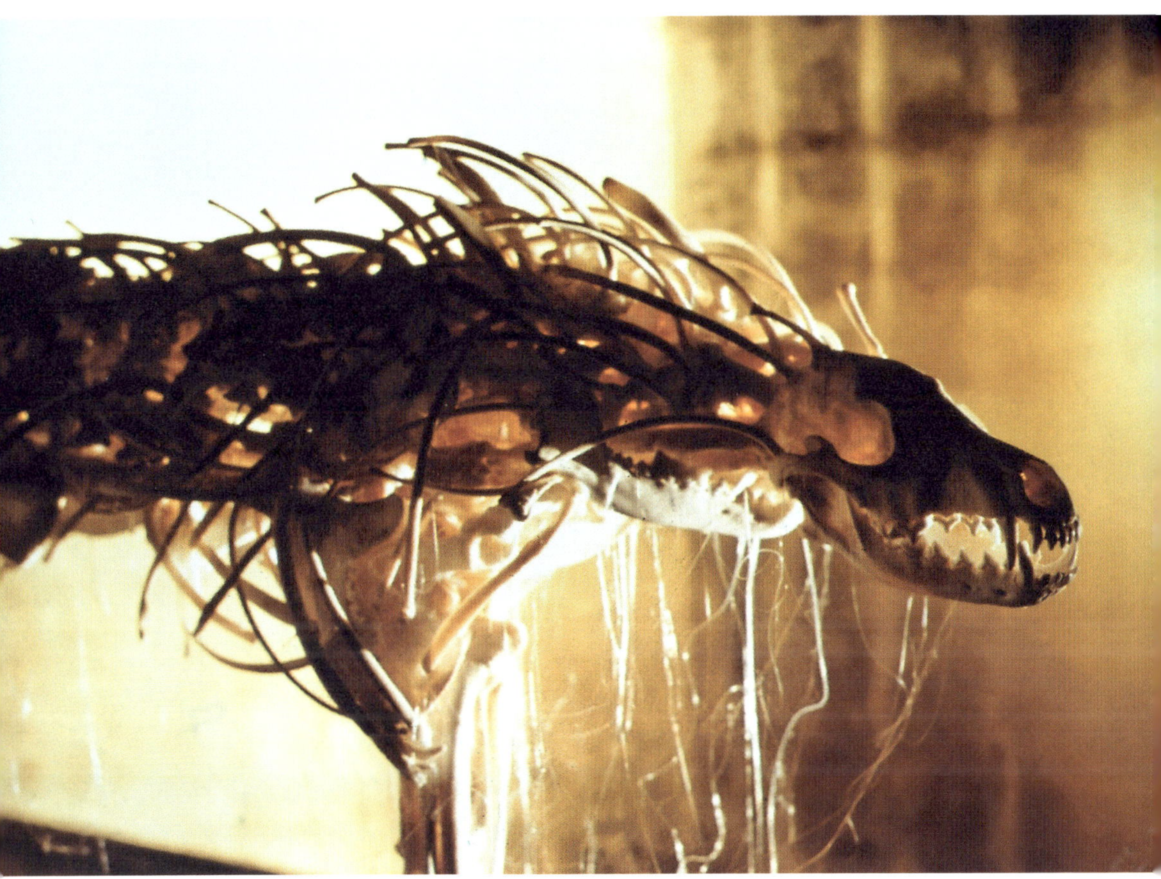

Edward Poitras (Métis, b. 1953), *Coyote's Big House*, 1995. Installation at the Canadian Pavilion, 1995 Venice Biennale. Coyote bones, hot wax glue, gilded panels. Photo © Gerald McMaster.

world. But, guess what, both halves were wrong. Parenthetically speaking, sure, once in a while some boat from half A landed in half B, or vice versa, and sometimes they even stayed for a while, but nothing really came of it.

And remember we're not just talking about people here: plants and microbes and animals lived separately for eons. What changed everything wasn't the first Columbus voyage, but the second, and soon they stopped counting.

Anyway, in 1492 the two halves of the world became permanently, irretrievably connected. It was the most consequential and profound event in human history, and created the world we know today. Contact changed everything, and we are still coming to terms with it. Based in large part on the massive transfer of wealth from the Americas, Europe—which a few centuries earlier was something of a backwater in what was known as the known world—quickly became home to the most powerful empires in human history. The Atlantic slave trade decimated Africa and further enriched Europe. Tens of millions of people in the Western Hemisphere, having no immunity to microbes that had never existed there before, died of the most widespread pandemic the world had ever seen. Corn and tomatoes and tobacco and potatoes, all Indian technologies, spread throughout the planet. It wasn't all death from diseases and wholesale murder and plundering the likes of which one rarely sees, although it was mostly that. It was also less brutal exchanges that produced new ways of thinking both here and over there. We became Indians, living in America. For a brief time in the early eighteenth century, we were actually called Americans by the English colonists. But we lost that, too, which I always thought was a drag because it's a better name for us than Indians or Natives or whatever. Lately, I've tried to popularize Reds, but that seems to be going nowhere fast.

To wrap up the depressing part, the biological invasion was at least initially nobody's fault. It was just a horrible thing that was going to happen sooner or later, and made possible a colonialism that looked different from other colonialisms at the time.

The stunning inequality of that exchange is what presents us with difficult problems. And there are very particular, very specific, unique problems that make the Indian question so difficult. European colonialism ruled most of the world for centuries, and even after it stopped directly ruling the world, it still ran big, huge chunks of it for a long time after that using the gauzy curtain of neocolonialism. By the mid twentieth century, most of Asia and Africa had at least bad nation states with less than perfect governments and armies and air forces and a seat at the United Nations. But in the Americas, that never happened. Yes, there are Indian nations of a kind, with sometimes real power, and yes, there's a province in Canada with autonomy, but colonialism in the Americas never allowed a result like China or India or Zimbabwe. Now, I'm not suggesting that modern nation states are the solution to our problems, or that most Indian people want such a thing now. I'm only pointing out a circumstance that is unique to us and different from other colonized people. And I think it explains why the discussions over the last several days about so many things just don't fit our experience.

So unless you can persuade me Europe would have become rich anyway, the Atlantic slave trade wasn't one of the major events of the last thousand years, and that wealth and technologies from America didn't change the world, then I'm going to insist that the Indian experience is at the very center of how the world we live in today came to be. When James Luna tells a story about a member of his tribe who was sent to Rome in the nineteenth century, he is telling an Indian story, but it is also an Italian story.

The Work We Have to Do

Native people insist on maintaining that difference in a way that is sometimes baffling to others. As my comrade Jolene Rickard (Tuscarora) so memorably wrote, though it may seem we've been pushed to the water's edge—dispossessed of nearly all of our homelands, populations, and wealth—instead of surrender, we've drawn a line on the sand. In front of us is the seemingly unstoppable dispossession machine, at our backs the roar of pounding surf, and Native people calculate the odds, nod to each other, and say, When do we attack?

But what is the value of that difference? I think it means that we have all kinds of things to offer. We see things differently. We come from a different place. For all the centuries of colonialism, for all the ways in North

America we've come to believe racist lies draped in romanticism, for all the times it may seem like we're vacationing on that beach instead of drawing a line on it, or serving as lifeguards for the colonists, the thing is we still come from a different place with a different history. The land question just won't go away, and neither will we.

The work we have to do to contribute to any serious dialogue is partly about confronting the anti-intellectualism in our own communities. It means giving up on the Indian belief that our people are always out there fighting colonialism, instead of being divided. It means acknowledging the vast differences even within the U.S. Indian world, which is all I can pretend to speak about. The Storr symposium took a lot of hits over the past four days about the narrowness of their representation, but the same thing could be said of us today. Our conference cannot pretend to represent the indigenous people of the Americas. It is as narrow with its own social and economic networks as any other. All we can do is try to be transparent about what we are doing here.

So *Vision, Space, Desire* is part of a larger ongoing effort for Indians to be present in the world. Success by Luna, Belmore, or this symposium won't be measured by how many Indians are in Venice or Kassel next time. It will be measured by something much harder to quantify, which is how much we contribute to the broader dialogue. Our presence in the global salon and its exhibitions, debates, arguments, and parties may seem important, but I would suggest that alone isn't success either. What really matters isn't the numbers or particular outcome, but whether we can build new understandings of what it means to be human in the twenty-first century. It isn't about us talking and you listening, it's about an engagement that moves our collective understanding forward.

Wednesday night, nonstop JFK to Venice, Delta flight 150. A bunch of us are on this flight, me, Gerald, Edgar Heap of Birds (Cheyenne/Arapaho), Jolene Rickard, Alan Michelson (Mohawk). We're approaching Europe, it's dawn, the lights are out, we're flying east. Rosa Martinez said something the other day about believing in chance, and Rob Storr, who will curate the Biennale in 2007, talked about Delmore Schwartz and the redemptive power of movies, which reminded me about the night before at JFK, when our researcher Rebecca Trautmann said, "Look, there's Liza Minnelli." And it was either Liza Minnelli or her exact double. So I knew that probably meant something, but I didn't know what.

So anyway, here we are on Delta 150. I'm listening to tunes, the flash music player is set on random so the zeros and ones are playing DJ, and they select Eva Cassidy. The song is "Over the Rainbow," Judy Garland's signature tune. I listen as the late, great Eva Cassidy steals this song from Liza Minnelli's mother. Which gets me to thinking about rainbows, something I don't generally do a whole lot, and remembering that my museum has crystal prisms built into its vast rotunda, which create rainbows on the walls when planets line up or something. (Note to self: find out if other museums manufacture rainbows.) I'm thinking about how much I love to fly even though I am terrified of air turbulence, and about how sappy that song makes me feel, and how happy I am to be alive in this century despite how truly horrible things are. And how glad I am that this dreadful year is finally over. One of the worst ever, I think, in the last thousand years.

That might be an exaggeration.

Anyway, the song ends, and Joy Division's "Love Will Tear Us Apart" comes on, and I decide to turn that off and wait for this lousy thing they call breakfast. And so we land in Venice, and at baggage claim somebody tells me that Rob Storr was on the same flight. So I'm thinking about how we've been flying across the ocean together, eight miles high, and here we are at the baggage claim, and thinking about all the potential for embarrassment this trip affords us. I am famous in my little crowd for saying that we are not ready for Prime Time, no, we shouldn't do it, whatever it is. And what I think was really terrific is none of us knew what was going to happen in this next week.

Paul Chaat Smith (Comanche) is an associate curator at the National Museum of the American Indian and a writer whose work is focused on contemporary North American Indian culture and politics.

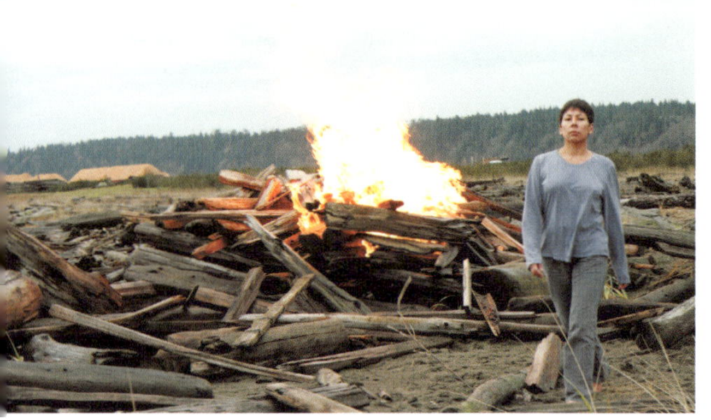

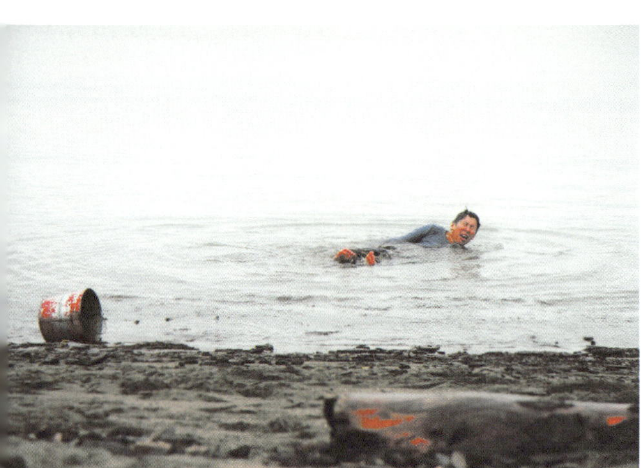

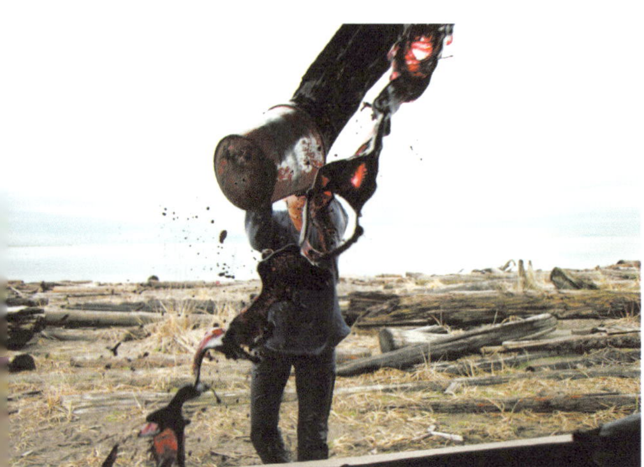

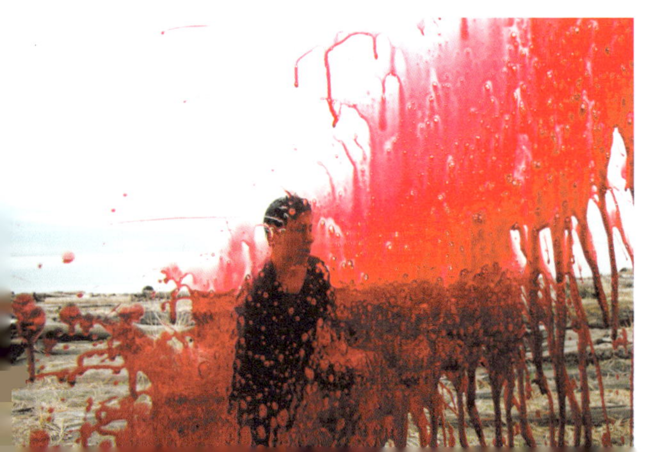

Rebecca Belmore (Anishinabe, b. 1960),
Fountain, 2005. Production Stills.
Photos by José Ramón González.
Images courtesy of the Morris and
Helen Belkin Art Gallery.

JEAN FISHER

"New Contact Zones": A Reflection

The title of this panel, for which I am serving as moderator, "New Contact Zones," has a particular resonance in a debate about forms of exchange between indigenous cultures and the global cultural and political sphere. Contact zones imply the existence of fairly distinct cultural spaces separated by an interface of potential interaction, recalling the histories of first contact between indigenous and European colonial cultures—confrontations between seemingly incommensurable worldviews in which one had to cede ground to the aggressive will of the other. That indigenous worldviews have survived despite centuries of enforced cession testify to the power of the local to embrace cultural difference and contradiction without relinquishing fundamentally sustainable concepts, presenting a fertile ground for developing new artistic and intellectual models of resistance to globalizing forces of homogenization and commodification.

As an outsider, I can say nothing of the dynamics of contemporary art practices internal to indigenous societies as they might articulate around differing historical trajectories, filiations to community and territory, degrees of urbanization, and acculturation to dominant national society. Regarding dynamics with external national cultures, it is a truism that indigenous art practices have long been circumscribed by what nowadays is termed "branded culture"—culture interpreted, packaged, and mobilized to serve the ideological or economic ends of the nation-state. The aesthetic and intellectual capital that the National Museum of the American Indian (NMAI) has gathered around it, however, represents a radical change in this dynamic; no more ceding to the demands of national culture, rather a desire, as James Luna (Luiseño) put it, "to lead and not be led," to shape the direction of cultural debates, not to be shaped by them. If this cannot be advanced through an indifferent national culture, then, presupposing that there is a consensus among indigenous cultural workers that insularity is not the way forward—a point emphasized in discussion by Cheyenne artist Edgar Heap of Birds—it makes sense to seek other spaces and alliances in a wider cultural field. The question becomes, what might be the enabling discourses, pathways, and vectors?

From the complex issues raised by the NMAI conference, I should like to sketch out, somewhat crudely, two themes. First, a question raised in preliminary discussions by the conference organizers and subsequently by various participants: what are the limitations of postcolonial and postmodern debates in the indigenous context? To clarify this is to clear a space for what Loretta Todd (Métis/Cree), more than ten years ago, called a "scholarship of our own" whose pathways were of indigenous intellectuals' choosing.[1] And second, a vital question raised by Gerald McMaster (Plains Cree and member of the Siksika Nation) in his introduction: how might indigenous subjectivity translate into political and artistic agency in the global sphere?

The Existing Discursive Field

A general consensus holds that indigenous peoples occupy an experiential and critical terrain that continues to be engaged in anti-colonial and neo-colonial struggles—notably, juridical recognition of cultural, territorial, and political sovereignty—while simultaneously grappling with more generalized postcolonial issues. Among the most widely known postcolonial commentaries, few address indigenous contexts, so how are they to be negotiated? Notwithstanding local circumstances, anti-colonial critique and postcolonial theory address rather different concerns. The former sees a world of antagonisms and hierarchical distinctions, and tends to be polarized around a rhetoric of victim and victimizer, exploiter and exploited, inevitably leaning toward cultural essentialism (nationalist or nativist). Aside from the problems of binarism and victimry, it also elides complex identificatory processes like the psychic ambivalence of desire and dread between self and other so compelling in postcolonial theory and so ably addressed in the work of Kent Monkman. Postcolonial theory, evolved largely by diasporan intellectuals in the wake of the collapse of militant liberation movements, refuses confrontational divisions in favor of discursive practices that speak of pluralized identities, border-crossings, and cultural hybridity. It is nonetheless criticized for privileging cultural and textual analysis over social, political, and historical realities.

For the indigenous subject filiated to community (a term that also needs unpacking), the nation-state is not the transcendental entity that, in Terry Eagleton's words, "incarnates culture" for the national subject.[2] On the contrary, the indigenous subject has historically been in critical and antagonistic relation to the representations of national (settler) society. These representations constitute the indigenous as the outside while disavowing its reality as the pivotal inside, which in part accounts for what Jolene Rickard (Tuscarora) describes as indigenous absence on both national and international stages. If for metropolitan postmodernism, however, migration, globalization, and the state's ceding of the public sphere to privatization have made indeterminate those traditional notions of belonging, civility, and subjectivity once thought to be secure and unified, where does the absented but filiated indigenous subject fit into the discussion?

One crucial point of contention involves the definition of culture itself and how the subject is constituted in it, a point astutely raised in a previous essay by Shanna Ketchum (Navajo).[3] As Ketchum and several conference participants confirmed, indigenous societies have been hostage to the anthropological idea of culture as a "finite and whole way of life" that derives from Eurocentric perceptions and value judgments. Under the objectifying processes of colonialism, cultural identities become frozen in a metaphysic of essences. This view inscribes the trajectory of early modernist primitivism as well as the more recent multicultural conflation of culture with ethnicity that ignores hierarchical relations of power. It affects the indigenous subject insofar as he or she is pushed toward nostalgia for, or an enactment of, past identities, which, for the national culture, conveniently distracts attention from the political realities of the present. Rickard sees this all-pervasive primitivism as the contestatory terrain of artist James Luna, seeking to reclaim indigenous subjectivity to contemporary reality. Likewise, postmodernism fails the indigenous subject in its valorization of multicultural diversity and decentered subjectivity at the expense of "community, tradition, rootedness, and solidarity."[4] As Donald and Rattansi point out, "the potential of such different communal traditions … as rivals to the dominant *national* culture in generating and legitimating beliefs, values and behaviour was disavowed," such that multiculturalism remained within the "political logic of assimilationism."[5] In notable distinction from this logic, many indigenous artists and intellectuals have effectively practiced in both Western academia and Native communities without apparent loss of subjective integrity. Paradoxically, these very dismissed categories of belonging have now returned to haunt the privileged West, both in the rise of fundamentalisms and the voided space of the communal, recently recognized by more socially conscious strands of contemporary art practice.

One challenge to the anthropological definition of culture comes from postcolonial debates, which propose that it is the differences between cultures—the hierarchical play of lack and plenitude, asymmetrical economic and political status—that *produce* culture: all cultures are hybrid because they are produced through *relations of difference*. To follow this path of reasoning is to shift the argument away from immutable essences, from culture as what "expresses the identity of a community" toward culture as the "processes, categories and knowledges through which communities are defined as such."[6] Is this transformative view of culture more adequate to the reality of indigenous cultures in which, as Nancy Marie Mithlo (Chiricahua Apache) argues, tradition (in contrast to Eurocentricism's temporalization of culture under the mantra of "progress") is understood as intimately bound synchronically into the discursive construction of the contemporary?

Concerning Agency, Spaces, and Vectors

Do these transformative processes necessarily produce cultural hybridity? Stuart Hall's critique of Homi Bhabha's widely disseminated vision of hybridity as the unstable occupation of an ambivalent in-between space precisely rests on the question of political agency and cultural intervention. Hall argues that if the in-between "enunciative space" is ambivalent, then it cannot be a constituted space or position from which a subject can speak. Political agency demands that a subject take a position, however contingent: without agency, there can be no intervention.[7]

The position from which an individual speaks is not reducible to identity, which gives us no purchase on the issue of political agency as the power to act and effect cultural change. People experience the world from particular positions: they speak to and from particular histories and geographies that present perspectives on reality that are different from others. As Rickard emphasizes, this space of culture—memory, home, belonging, identification—constructs subjectivity as filiation, or affiliation, to a specific community, its values and continuity. Positions, unlike identities, may be plural, mobile, and strategic. In this regard, postcolonial diasporan debates about cultural hybridity offer little to the contemporary indigenous subject whose chosen positions may be more tactical than ambivalent. Is it, then, more useful to think of contemporary indigenous subjects as "constituted" and knowingly engaged in an agonistic "war of position" among diverse cultural possibilities according to expediency and opportunity?

Agency perhaps should not be thought of in terms of individual will but as the fields of activity in which subjects and communities map and position themselves with varying degrees of mobility relative to relations of power. According to Lawrence Grossberg, if subjectivity constitutes "homes" as places of attachment, "agency constitutes strategic installations ...[it] involves participation and access, the possibility of moving into particular sites of activity and power, and of belonging to them in such a way as to be able to enact their powers."[8] In this sense NMAI's presence in Venice becomes a strategic occupation of a particular site of power in which the indigenous artist or curator is a potential vector of intervention. As Paul Chaat

Smith (Comanche) insists, "every place is an Indian place." In which case, should indigenous peoples have a responsibility to seize opportunities to occupy and stake their own claim to sites of activity and power? If, as Aboriginal curator Brenda Croft points out, the national culture is resistant to promoting artists as both international and indigenous, then artists need to consolidate their local base with international exchange. At the same time, as Mithlo emphasizes, the artistic and philosophical terms of any such engagement must be reconfigured in ways that no longer take their cue reactively from the mainstream but from the more proactive perspective of what she calls "alternative knowledge systems" and Native ways of doing things.

Despite its assimilationist tendencies, multiculturalism enabled a breach in the wall of the hegemonic art system in which inclusion of "others" in a space still governed by Eurocentric privilege offered a strategic moment; but it fell prey to a visibility contingent on the display of ethnic markers. Nonetheless, artists and intellectuals took this opportunity to insinuate other narratives of history from previous repressed cultural spaces that challenged the Eurocentric master narrative and the museum as its privileged site of a triumphalist art historical and evolutionist scholarship of collecting, classifying, and interpreting. The dominant center-periphery model, if not eradicated, has at least been weakened by the proliferation of multiple, global sites of art that do not all aspire to mimic Western formats. In Robert Storr's conference, both Gerardo Mosquera and Vasif Kortun described curatorial projects that were more focused on evolving strategies of artistic exchange with local community, echoing Mithlo's description of the way NA3 connected with the life-world of local Venetians. These projects highlight the importance of attending to spectatorship and how museums and art practices construct audiences. The work of, say, Heap of Birds, Rebecca Belmore (Anishinabe), and Alan Michelson (Mohawk) demonstrates the possibility of speaking to the universal through an articulation of indigenous hermeneutics with international artistic languages. Thus, what has emerged, as Mithlo suggests, is an indigenous cosmopolitan consciousness connected to global concerns but interpreted through localized systems of knowledge whose art practices are neither folkloric nor postmodern. The complementary support of indigenous philosophic and art historical scholarship, disseminated, as suggested by Salah Hassan, through diverse networks and publications, is necessary, as Rickard says, to deconstruct the colonial space and restructure an indigenous space that values its past achievements as well as forging artistic and political agencies in dialogue with others resistant to the flattening effect of globalization. As a vital center of scholarship and dissemination, NMAI would function not as the repository of the past but as a living archive.

Jean Fisher is Professor of Fine Arts and Transcultural Studies at Middlesex University, London, England.

NOTES

1. Loretta Todd, "What More Do They Want?" in Gerald McMaster and Lee-Ann Martin, eds., *INDIGENA: Contemporary Native Perspectives* (Vancouver: Douglas & McIntyre, 1992), 76.

2. Terry Eagleton, *The Idea of Culture* (Oxford: Blackwell, 2000), 7.

3. Shanna Ketchum, "Native American Cosmopolitan Modernism(s). A Re-articulation of Presence through Time and Space," *Third Text* 19: 4 (July 2005): 357–64.

4. Eagleton, 13.

5. James Donald and Ali Rattansi, eds., *"Race," Culture and Difference* (London: Sage Publications and the Open University, 1992), 2.

6. Ibid., 4.

7. See *Locations of Culture,* a discussion of postcolonial culture between Homi Bhabha, Stuart Hall, and Paul Gilroy (London: ICA video, 1993).

8. Lawrence Grossberg, "Identity and Cultural Studies: Is That All There Is?" in Stuart Hall and Paul Du Gay, eds., *Questions of Cultural Identity* (London: Sage Publications, 1996), 99.

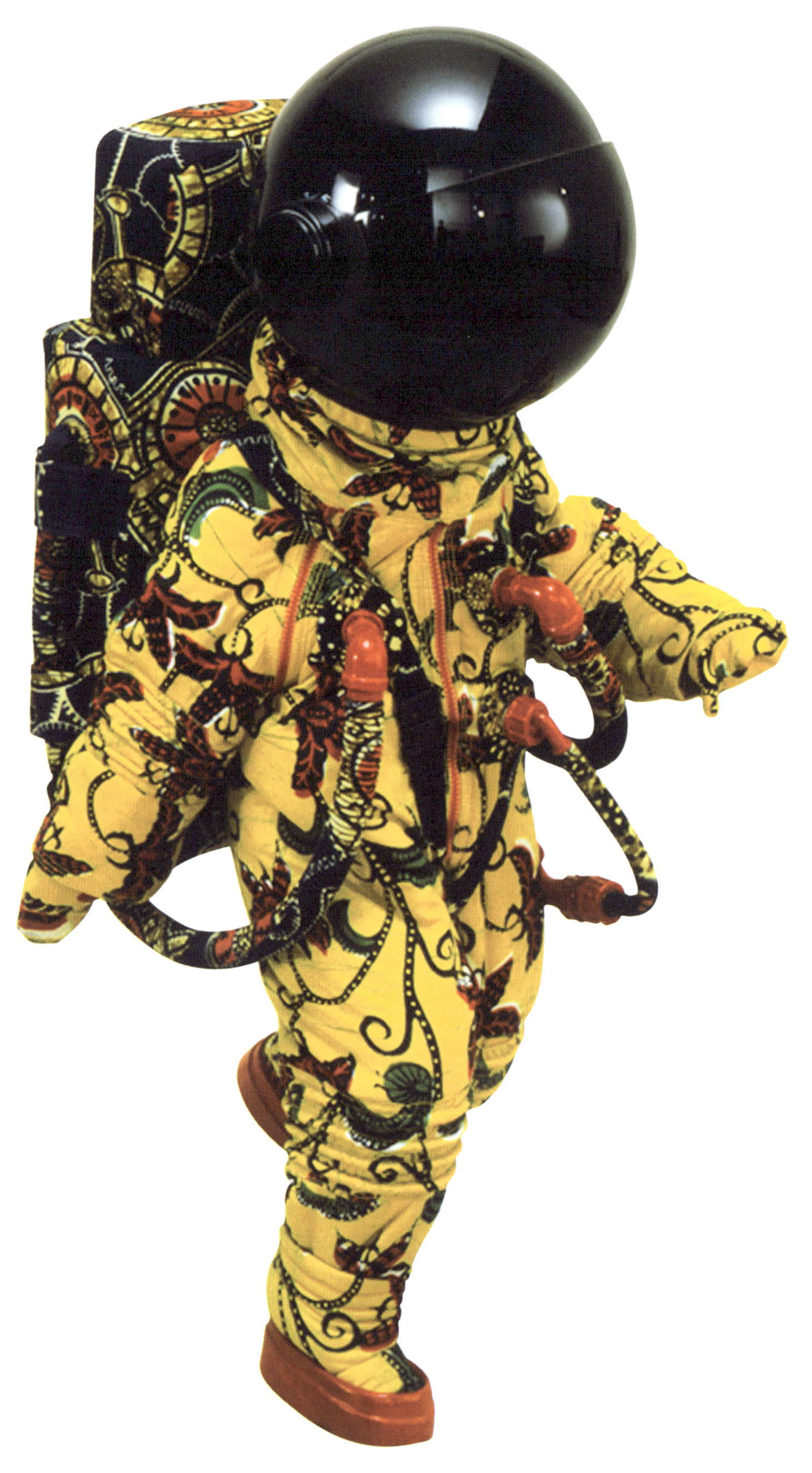

SALAH HASSAN

Why Venice? Why Visions?

I was invited to this conference at a time when I felt my brain had almost turned into a fossil after five years of a stint as Chair of the Art History Department at Cornell University. Those of you who have had these kinds of administrative responsibilities know very well that scholarly research and writing become the first victims in this process.

It is a pleasure to be here because this is one way of reinvigorating or at least trying to, can we say, un-fossilitize. When I received the invitation, I thought about what would be the best way to address some of the issues that Jean Fisher just elaborated in terms of the questions put forward for us by the organizers, and I decided to give a presentation entitled "Why Venice? Why Visions?" in which my own experience of working in Venice would be helpful as a focus. I could use it as a case study and elaborate on many of the questions and issues from a practical point of view.

I will concentrate on our experience of creating the Forum for African Arts, which I will explain for those of you who are not familiar with it. And, more specifically, I will discuss the initiation in Venice of what we called Africa in Venice. As a result of that effort, we have had at least three interventions so far in the last Venice Biennale. Since our initiative was a consequence of a deliberate and tireless effort to inaugurate an African presence at the 49th Venice Biennale (2001), which was about three Biennales ago,

Yinka Shonibare (British/Nigerian, b. 1962), *Vacation* (detail), 2000. Dutch wax printed cotton textile, fiberglass, plastic. Courtesy of the artist and Stephen Friedman Gallery, London.

questions may arise as to its location and its strategy, especially in light of the considerable expense and bureaucracy involved (and Venice is probably one of the most expensive and difficult places on earth to do exhibits). I think the discussion of the past three days of the Storr conference explains not only those practical or logistical difficulties but also how difficult it is to change the minds of the people who are involved in the Venice Biennale—the organizers behind the scenes. Why Venice, why visions? The answers to these questions are complex and multilayered and range from the straightforward fact of the Venice Biennale's continued significance in contemporary art to much deeper issues of history and the realities of contemporary cultural relations.

I hope that my focus on the African presence at the Venice Biennale will provide some comparative perspective to the Native American presence—another marginalized group. The African presence has always been minimal and sporadic. Since the Biennale's inception, only one African country, Egypt, has maintained a national pavilion. Egypt was one of the earliest non-European nations to establish a pavilion (beginning with the second Biennale) and has had a long-standing awareness of the Biennale's significance as an international cultural forum. Although many of my Egyptian friends said to me jokingly—and if you know Egyptians, you know they like to joke a lot—that the establishment of the pavilion was not necessarily due to an awareness, it was actually the fact that King Fu'ad and Prince Farouk had some Italian women lovers at the time.

For a brief period, before it was ostracized for its racial laws, South Africa also presented its artists in Venice. Otherwise, throughout its history, only two traveling exhibitions of African art made it to the Venice Biennale, one in the 45th Biennale (1993) and the other in the 46th (1995). Both exhibitions were organized by Western curators and were in many ways marginal to the main events of the Biennale, although one of the African exhibitions won the First Exhibitor's Medal at the 45th Biennale. It is equally noteworthy that as recently as the 48th Biennale in 1999, which was just before we intervened, of the more than one hundred artists invited to *d'APERTutto*, the main exhibition organized by the artistic director, Harald Szeemann, only three were African (two were white South Africans and the other was a black South African).

On a certain level, therefore, our Africa in Venice initiative is part of an effort to remedy the virtual absence of Africans in the Venice Biennale—and hopefully in other significant international cultural forums of its kind. Some may wonder why such forums and exhibitions in general are so important as opposed to text or other means of presenting African art. And Africans themselves love arts, so why Venice? Why can't you just invest this money in Africa? In fact, this question was posed to us by philanthropic foundations that supported our project. I think the Ford and Rockefeller foundations were the exception in this case, and also the Prince Claus Fund, but most organizations that we approached had this kind of benevolent, charitable mentality that you have to do your project in Africa, poor Africa. I am not against doing something in Africa, and, in fact, we did some projects in Africa. But I wanted to do this project—or we wanted to do it, if I speak collectively for the group that is behind it—in Venice. The answer to me, in general, is that if you don't exhibit, you don't exist. Exhibitions remain exemplars of how art history is produced; they are the building blocks of art history and therefore crucial in moving out from the private to the public domain.

In the cultural politics of the past two centuries, exhibitions and the curatorial practices behind them constitute the most enduring and perhaps the most powerful means of selecting, staging, and ultimately canonizing art. As Walter Grasskamp has observed, "Historiography, including art historiography, is only possible if a few events are selected from the chaos and peddled."[1] Exhibitions and forums for showcasing artistic creativity are part of art history's strategy to transform this chaos into more manageable units out of which it creates the semblance of a coherent historic narrative. Needless to say, this strategy involves not only art historians and critics, but also an entire cultural machine comprised of an array of culture managers and brokers, including curators, patrons, museums, art galleries, art dealers, agents, and collectors, as well as the most well-attended showcases of contemporary art.

The Venice Biennale provides this increasingly global machine with a ready-made package of what is considered to be the latest trends on the international art scene. Curators, museum directors, gallery owners, art critics, and other specialists from virtually every part of the planet descend on Venice for a glimpse of this official currency—with undoubtedly significant consequences for artists and cultural constituencies with any interest in the international contemporary art scene. Given this fact, it becomes particularly interesting that African artists are absent. For while the paucity of African national pavilions in Venice may be explained by economic reasons, or the lack of consistent national policies that give priority to culture, these reasons do not explain the absence of African artists from the invitational exhibitions at the Biennale for which the artistic director is responsible.

This omission of African artists from the Biennale invitational exhibitions, it seems to us, speaks to reluctance, even unwillingness, on the part of curators to acknowledge these artists and their provenance as part of contemporary art and our moment in history. Whereas in the distant past it could be argued that little was known in the West about these artists, such an excuse no longer holds, since many of them now work and practice internationally along with their contemporaries from elsewhere, producing work that is concerned with issues quite analogous to those that currently occupy other artists. It is difficult to name or quantify this unwillingness, yet it fits into a pattern that appears to change very little, even as these artists become more visible in the international scene, and new bodies of knowledge are generated around their practice.

I want to say here that books on contemporary art that included contemporary African art had been published. Our magazine, *Nka: Journal of Contemporary African Art*, has been established since 1994, and even the traditional African art magazine, I must say, has changed its focus and has actually started to include contemporary African art. So a body of knowledge in text was there. Yet in 1997, both the 47th Venice Biennale and Documenta X in Kassel, Germany—Europe's two most important surveys of international contemporary art—provided striking illustrations of the non-inclusion of African artists. Not a single African artist was included in the

Biennale, which Germano Celant organized as a survey—and, mind you, this is a survey of contemporary art in the late twentieth century—under the banner *Future, Present, Past*. Effectively the curator's position was that African artists had no place in any narrative of contemporary art in the late twentieth century despite all their contributions to contemporary culture, even in the West. At Documenta X, Catherine David made last-minute efforts to invite African artists, but this appeared almost like an afterthought in an exhibition supposedly devoted to issues of globalization and internationalism in the visual arts.

The 2nd Johannesburg Biennale in South Africa (also 1997) provided a graphic contrast. Artistic director Okwui Enwezor and his team of international curators presented an inclusive, comprehensive narrative of contemporary art with sufficient evidence of the presence and strength of African artists as part of a global contemporary culture. The sharp disparity with the events in Venice and Kassel makes it clear that the absence of African artists in international space at the time did not result from lack of knowledge of their existence or any inadequacy in the work but rather points to a persistent shortcoming in the political will of cultural brokers and managers in the West to locate them alongside artists from other parts of the world.

This was the backdrop against which we curated *Authentic/Ex-Centric: Africa in and out of Africa* in 2001 as our first intervention in Venice. The exhibition was held at the Fondazione Levi, and I had the pleasure of curating it with my colleague Olu Oguibe, who was at the time also co-editor of *Nka: Journal of Contemporary African Art. Authentic/Ex-Centric* featured seven prominent African artists: Willem Boshoff from South Africa, Maria Magdalena Campos-Pons from Cuba, Godfried Donkor from Ghana, Rachid Koraïchi from Algeria, Berni Searle from South Africa, Zineb Sedira from Algeria, and Yinka Shonibare from Nigeria and the United Kingdom. I mention the nationality of these people just to point to the fact that the exhibit was not a pavilion for Africa, it was a thematic show developed within certain ideas to highlight a certain movement. These accomplished artists are all working within the conceptual mode in painting, sculpture, photography, video, and multimedia installations. All live and work between Africa and Western centers of artistic production, which was very important to the exhibition theme.

We also made it a priority to produce books and leave behind a legacy in text. *Authentic/Ex-Centric: Conceptualism in Contemporary African Art* was published in conjunction with the exhibition, and since then we have come out with two other books. We insisted that everything connected with the project—even our banners—be made with a level of excellence, and we were adamant about having a central place in Venice for the exhibition. We cannot afford to reproduce the marginality or marginalization of Africa within Venice.

Space within the Arsenale or the Giardini, of course, was not available to us. We paid some $70,000 to rent the centrally located Fondazione Levi for a very short period of time. And I must acknowledge here that it is due to the help of many Italian friends that we managed to do this. It would have been impossible to accomplish our goal without the support of people who believed in our project and mission. I found it a valuable lesson to realize that within societies that we perceive as hegemonic are people who work against the grain or the mainstream and are our allies in this kind of venture.

Ensconced in our highly visible location, we made the biggest banner in Biennale history. In fact, the authorities intervened and told us that we must shrink it, which we did. But at least we had it on the opening day, so anybody on the canal at the time managed to see it.

The word "authentic" in the exhibition title references the responses of some of the artists to the politics of representation as well as to paradigms of discourse that objectify African and other cultures. It plays on cultural determinism and the demand for "authenticity" and the exotic that continue to frame the acknowledgment and reception of African contemporaneity outside the continent. And as I said then, we were really working against the grain because the demand at that time for artists from Africa was oriented to the less educated, as close to the bush as possible, or for the fine painter types and so forth of the type found in the collection now known as the Jean Pigozzi Collection. Several of the works in our exhibition reexamined such notions of originality and authenticity, and spoke back to them.

The term "ex-centric" addresses other realities of cultural politics as they affect African artists within and outside Africa. It also points to issues of cross-cultural and transnational aesthetics and consciousness within contemporary African art practice, especially since our exhibition reflected the reciprocal traffic of ideas and influences between Africa and other parts of the world. We also hoped to offer a glimpse of the ways in which African artists have interpreted and translated the aesthetic and social experiences of both historical and postcolonial Africa as part of a global sensitivity.

The works of the artists included in *Authentic/Ex-Centric* highlight conceptual interventions in contemporary African Art. Maria Magdalena Campos-Pons's *Spoken Softly with Mama*, part of a series of works titled *History of People Who Were Not Heroes*, addresses issues relating to the African diaspora, expatriation, gender, and race. Rachid Koraïchi's installation *Chemin des Roses* evokes travel and transcendence in Islamic Sufi thought. Willem Boshoff's installation continues his exploration of language and text, while Godfried Donkor exhumes repressed histories of the black presence in Europe. The exhibition also included video works by Berni Searle and Zineb Sedira. Yinka Shonibare was the magnet for the exhibit—and this is a strategy we tried to follow, to get a well-known artist to participate in the exhibit. His dealer at the time, Stephen Friedman, at first refused to allow Yinka to work with us, saying that he didn't want the artist to be part of an ethnic show. But Yinka resisted and agreed to be part of the exhibition.

And then, of course, we did the second intervention, which I must say was a step forward. *Fault Lines: Contemporary African Art and Shifting Landscapes*, which featured a range of African and African diaspora artists, was presented at the Arsenale as part of the 50th Venice Biennale in 2003. Artistic director Francesco Bonani actually included our exhibition, curated by Gilane Tawadros, as part of his five major shows. As I mentioned earlier, the help of supporters is important, and we are grateful to our friends within the Venice Biennale such as Chiara Bertola and Rosa Martinez.

And let me just conclude with the lessons that one learned. We insisted on doing every aspect of the project with the same standard of excellence. We hired a superb architect who happened to be a friend, Tom Postma, who was the fair designer for Art Basel Miami Beach 2005, and made sure that we had staff who could manage to work in the difficult spaces of Venice. The career of many of these artists skyrocketed, and we ourselves, as curators, were invited to do other shows. And, as I said, the success of the second exhibition was also important.

Salah Hassan is Chair of the Department of History of Art and Director of the Africana Studies and Research Center, Cornell University, Ithaca, New York. He is editor of Nka: Journal of Contemporary African Art *and consulting editor for* African Arts.

NOTES
1. Walter Grasskamp, "For Example, *Documenta*, or, How is Art History Produced?" in Reesa Greenberg et al, eds., *Thinking about Exhibitions* (New York: Routledge, 1996), 68.

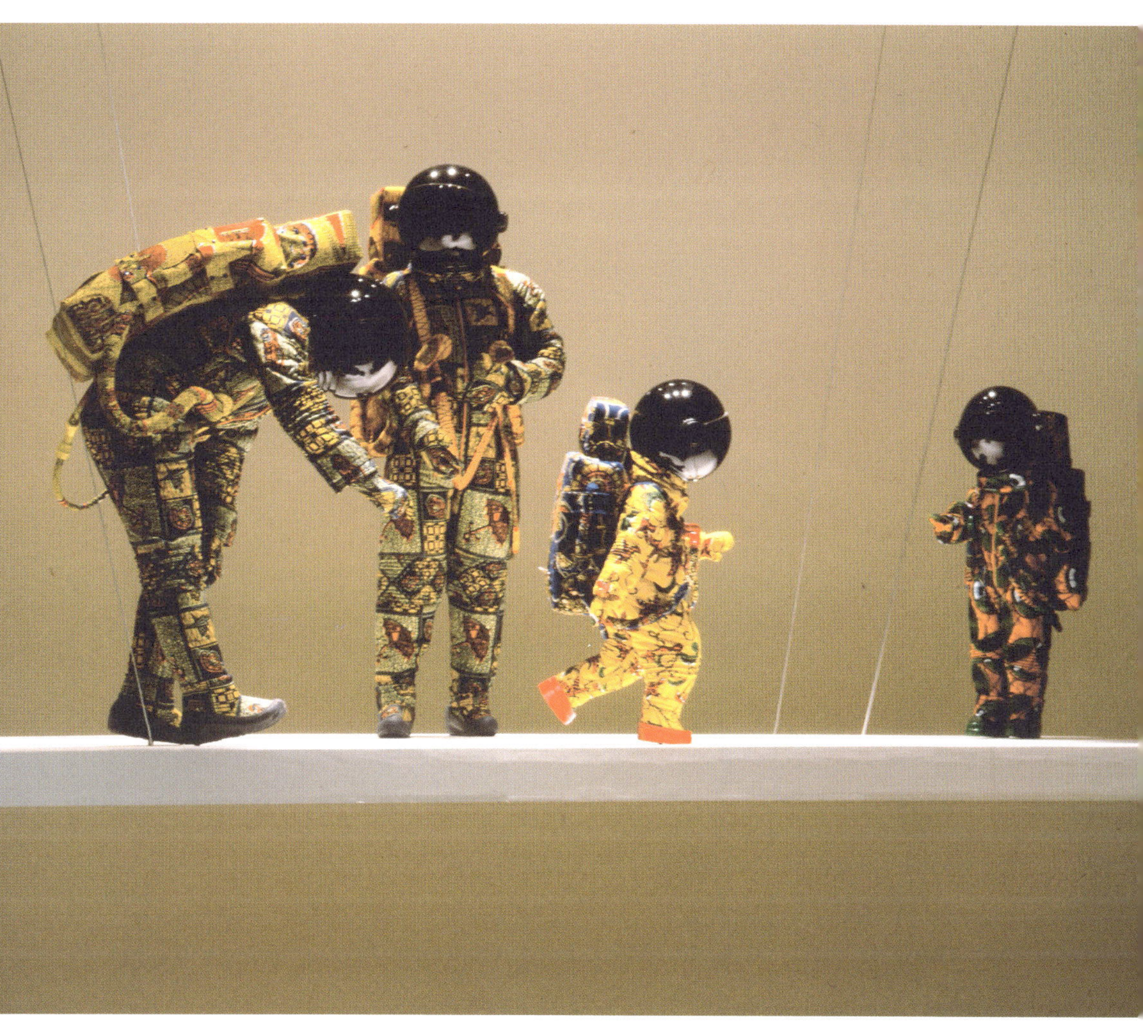

Yinka Shonibare (British/Nigerian, b. 1962), *Vacation*, 2000. Dutch wax printed cotton textile, fiberglass figures, plastic. Courtesy of the artist and Stephen Friedman Gallery, London.

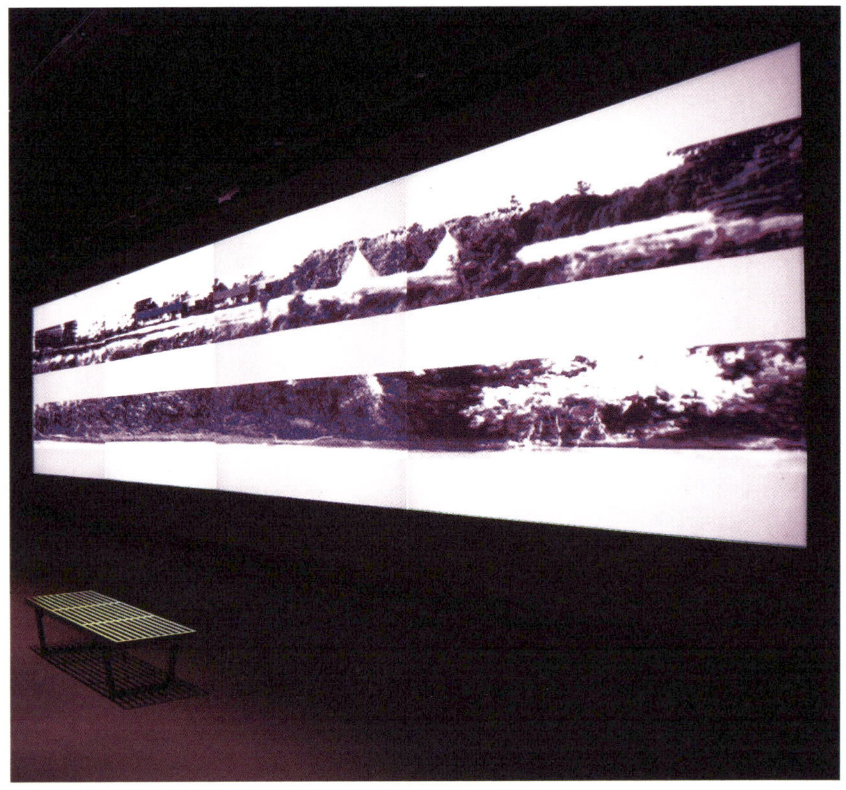

Alan Michelson (Mohawk, b. 1953), *TwoRow II*, 2005. Four-channel digital video with sound, 13 min. 5 sec., 275.6 x 1524 cm. Installation view, George Gustav Heye Center, National Museum of the American Indian, New York, New York. Photo by Gwendolen Cates. © Alan Michelson.

JOLENE RICKARD

THE LOCAL AND THE GLOBAL

Venice, 2005: a wall of water splashes to the floor inside the Canadian pavilion in the Giardini, acting as a liminal framing for *Fountain,* the performance piece by Rebecca Belmore. Off-site, in an equally impressive space, James Luna challenges an easily distracted audience with an installation and four-hour performance, *Emendatio.* It is not the first time that indigenous artists from the Americas have been in the Venice Biennale, but it is the first time that an indigenous woman represented a national space, specifically Canada. The intersection of both artists—one from Luiseño territories bordering Southern California and the other from Anishinabe territories, via Vancouver, British Columbia—provides this opportunity for reflection. Belmore's and Luna's art merits inclusion in international art exhibitions, but another dimension to their participation is equally provocative.

To fully embrace Luna's work, one has to understand the ongoing construction of the primitive, the exoticization of Native cultures, the impact of colonization, missionization, and the forms of performance and installation art. Although less overt in expressing an indigenous philosophy, Belmore's work is enriched by contemplating the possible connection to Anishinabe knowledge of the human condition due to transformation of water to blood. Belmore does not suppress the fact that her work is informed by her heritage and, simultaneously, the contemporary world. But one must ask whether Belmore's and Luna's specific history as indigenous people fits into the international biennial art world. Some would argue that it is just about art, and not about Native art. I argue that it is about both, in order to avoid the complete flattening of the local within a global context. This is a dangerous argument, and I am struck by the struggle articulated by curators Wu Hung and Gao Minglu during the Storr symposium. Their subjectivity as Chinese curators focusing on Chinese art is not questioned. The question of separating out the specificity of Chinese philosophy and history from the artwork is not considered; rather academia and non-Chinese curators are preparing themselves to understand the cultural and political terrain of Chinese aesthetics. Yet, as Wu Hung points out, even with 1,300,000,000 Chinese returning the gaze, there is still the tendency to flatten the local. What kind of reception does that signal for an acceptance of an indigenous local?

How Do We Make Small Work for Us?

The entire world is activated around trying to accommodate the emergent Chinese. There is no such global focus on the recognition of indigenous people or our art. While the Chinese have the largest population in the world, indigenous people have one of the smallest. If big works for the Chinese, how do we make small work for us?

The question may be about the idea of an indigenous presence too local for an international discussion, or perhaps the question is, Where does the presence of indigenity fit in an international art world that has thus far constructed Native American existence or reality as an absence? First, we must consider if the museum and the artwork space represent a valid and necessary site of negotiation. I view this as analogous to the negotiation for setting the agenda that takes place before a G8 or WTO economic summit.

If you are not in the negotiation to set the agenda, then your issues are never represented in the meeting. If indigenous artists are not recognized in the international dialogue as indigenous, we are aesthetically present, but we are invisible, colonial subjects. The reversal of postcolonial subjugation is complex in the Americas, since this is where we were framed as a colonial space. In my recent role as guest curator for the Smithsonian's National Museum of the American Indian in Washington, D.C., I felt like I was for a brief moment setting the agenda for the meeting. I took on this assignment because I believe in the necessary synchronicity between very public interventions such as NMAI's potential to reach millions of people per year and also the more selective audience before me here today.

I addressed the issue of invisibility in two installations as a curatorial intervention. The first was located in the *Our Peoples* exhibition, supported by the cryptic text of my collaborator Paul Chaat Smith, where I used hundreds of pre-Contact figures from the collection to stand in for the debate on how populated the Americas were in 1491, just before Contact. The point of the installation was not to create yet another meta-narrative or revisit the gaps of information caused by the multiple ruptures indigenous peoples in the Americas endured, but to acknowledge how diverse and populated the Americas were at this time. The back of the installation provides a luminous space for the figurines, creating a ghost-like presence. I wanted to provide the opportunity for the visitor to recognize or make the connection that our ancestors are still with us—therefore present, not erased. Information on individual figurines could be accessed from a computer within the gallery space. Although I view the provenance of each figure as important, their collective presence is the source of significance.

My second intervention on the invisibility of indigenous peoples in the Americas was in the entrance to the *Our Lives* exhibition, which is concerned with contemporary Native life. The installation features a media projection on a two-way mirror. Footage of people walking is projected through the mirror and a soundscape of light conversation surrounds visitors as they pass through the entry. Visitors are reflected in the mirror as if walking with the people in the media projection. The importance is in the ordinariness or commonality of the visitors and the Native people in the media piece. Visitors encountered text stating that anywhere you stand in the Americas, you could be standing next to an indigenous person. The experience was meant to be participatory, and to de-exoticize the notion of indigenous people today while reinforcing our contemporary presence. These installations create an opportunity to call for a shift in the imaginations of non-Native people to recognize our global presence as indigenous people.

The United Nations made a parallel attempt to raise the level of awareness about issues facing indigenous peoples worldwide when it declared the 1990s the Decade of Indigenous Peoples. Ultimately, the initiative was under-funded and did little to heighten consciousness of these issues within First World or developed nations. The question of nationhood puts indigenous artists at a disadvantage, given the basic formulation for biennial exhibitions that are organized around notions of nationhood. Ironically, even current postmodern and postcolonial framings referencing conditions of diaspora, dislocation, relocation, and exile are dependent on the formation of nationhood. The art world is still grappling with locating so-called Third World or non-Western art in a continuous way, and even the most inclusive critiques struggle with an articulation of where indigenity fits in the discussion.

Invisibility

Invisibility remains a key issue in the Americas and globally for indigenous people. And what do I mean by indigenous? In the Americas, there are thousands of different Native groups that self-define as Native nations, tribes, and/or communities. The important point is that most of these people foreground their heritage over more recent colonial interventions like the United States, Canada, Mexico, Brazil, and so forth. The struggle for autonomous nationhood embedded in a political discourse of sovereignty is a critical factor for the ongoing presence of indigenity in the Americas. Specifically, the expression of this idea spans from a self-authoring red card issued by the Haudenosaunee, or Iroquois (Six Nations), to the acceptance of identity cards or numbers issued by the government of the United States. Each colonial nation has a similar tracking device, but since America is the new, yet simultaneously declining, empire of the twenty-first century, it is a revelatory example of an ongoing colonial relationship. The red card signals a struggle to articulate a legal history and diplomatic relationship with a more recently formed United States.

I have here a red card issued by the Onondaga, embossed on the front with the great White Pine surrounded by the clans of the Six Nations. The holder's name, clan, and nation are typed inside, and the treaties articulating the relationship between the United States and the Haudenosaunee are listed on the back. It is important to note that the treaties listed on the red card have been ratified by the American legal system and therefore are part of the United States legal history. The defense of these treaties within the American courts forces the United States to recognize its own laws. The treaties are not our laws, but we negotiated these agreements when we still had bargaining power. Treaties are not negotiated with powerless peoples or nations, so these documents represent a balance of power at the time of their creation. They signify recognition by the United States of our claim to our land, customs, and traditions, expressed today by the Iroquois as sovereignty. The red cards are not part of our tradition, but were instigated by accommodation of the colonial settler, or the United States.

The red card stands in contrast to the Certificates of Degree of Indian Blood issued by the United States. These documents are tied to the ongoing debate in Native communities concerning the question of blood quantum as the means to determine Native identity. So important is the question of who is an Indian that an entire section of the *Our Lives* exhibition is devoted to it, ranging from the earliest debates about whether Indians had a soul and were human, documented in the letters of Bartolomé de las Casas (1484–1566), to the inclusion of photographs of a work by artist Hulleah Tsinhnahjinnie (Diné/Seminole/Muscogee) in which she stamps a federally issued identity number on her forehead as a statement of ongoing subjugation (*Would I Have Been a Member of the Nighthawk, Snake Society or Would I Have Been a Half-Breed Leading the Whites to the Full-Bloods*, 1991).

Documentation of James Luna's 1987 performance artwork *The Artifact Piece* anchors the identity panel, serving as a final comment on the relationship between the West and indigenous people. The museum as West in this case is a metaphor for the American Empire, with its desire to locate indigenous people as collected, catalogued, and contained—and ultimately vanished into the past. The ironic statement by Luna, whose physical presence overturns the notion that Native people's art is extinct, opens up the space to discuss the ongoing erasure of indigenity globally. Why is it important to retell the specific history?

On the other side of the exhibition panel, we focused on the multiple identities of Native staff from the museum and Native people in the Washington area. We had a media piece that made problematic the notion of blood quantum. A reference to the red card is meant to show that indigenous governments are still in some kind of political relationship with federal or colonial governments. Indigenous nations and communities within North America have been identified by scholar Gordon Brotherston as being part of a Fourth World. This Fourth World is not the same as the Hopi notion of the time of the Fourth World, but closer to the First World/Third World analogy used in discussion of the dichotomy between the developed and developing world. How is this information useful to an art world seeking universals? The discursive space in the arts needs to expand its notion of First World and Third World or developed and developing nations and acknowledge an indigenous space. This is not a rhetorical political position, but the subject of a large percentage of art coming from indigenous artists.

Today we cannot look at artwork without applying multiple readings of gender as central to analysis. What would that framing concept be as it applies to indigenous art? The core of my analysis has been how indigenous art communities communicate to the art world, the museum audience in Washington, D.C., and the attendees at this conference. I have not yet addressed an area that may very well be the most important—how indigenous artists address their own communities and other indigenous people. Where the early 1990s work of Luna, Tsinhnahjinnie, and others deconstructed a colonial space, the work today needs to reimagine an indigenous space. We need to make art for each other. We need to write for each other, and we need to do it on a global scale. The recent collaborations between First Nation artists in Canada and Aboriginal artists in Australia represent a potential template for the future. I am not suggesting that we operate in a hermeneutic bubble; rather, I think we need to articulate local knowledge globally. But the question of what indigenous artists bring to the insatiable appetite of the art world's craving for new ideas needs to be made visible.

The visibility begins with the simple recognition of our existence as discrete political and philosophical spaces throughout the world. The discovery or news is in the realization of our continued existence within modern nation-states. At the Storr Biennale conference and within current debate, the negative impact of globalization as a cultural or local knowledge flattener has been repeatedly cited. I do not think I need to retell the impact of the loss of local knowledge with the rise of the Cartesian model on women's authority in post-Renaissance Europe. As indigenous people, perhaps we face a similar circumstance in the form of globalization. In the face of this new shift, we indigenous people need to recognize our success.

The Insight of Continuity

The success is local and understood through specific examples. I turn to a 2005 work by Mohawk artist Alan Michelson for this example, but I should note that I believe Belmore's piece in this year's Biennale is also an articulation of this idea and is addressed in the essay that I wrote for the catalogue *Rebecca Belmore: Fountain*. Michelson's piece, titled *TwoRow II*, evokes both an object and a concept based on a seventeenth-century agreement between the Iroquois and European settlers. Michelson's artwork, which uses simultaneous panoramic video projections, is a contemporary reinterpretation of that original agreement, which was marked with a wampum belt. Michelson appropriated the visual structure of the historic Two Row Wampum Belt to represent the ongoing articulation of a principle between two peoples. The Two Row has been interpreted as a visual representation of mutual respect. The two purple bands represent the cultures—one European, one Mohawk—while the white area in between is the space that maintains the integrity of each purple boundary and represents the desire for peace.

For Iroquois people, the Two Row is a reminder about which path to follow. Often the Two Row is thought of as two swift streams, with canoes as symbols of our lives, reminding us that if we try to straddle both canoes, we will fall into the water. I do not interpret this literally; like most expressions in our culture, it is a metaphor. Falling into the water in this case is letting go of our culture. This symbol and hundreds more form a body of knowledge that has made it possible for Alan Michelson and me to continue to be Mohawk and Tuscarora people. We did this in the backyard of the wealthiest and most powerful empire in the modern age, which is, of course, America. We maintained our local knowledge and continued to think of our experience as human beings in relation to the Haudenosaunee principles of peace, power, and righteousness.

The newest empire is not a nation-state but the process of globalization. In this empire, every human being risks the flattening process. I argue that indigenous people globally do have something very important to contribute on the cusp of the twenty-first century. We have densely packed cultural survival kits that transfer knowledge from one generation to the next, despite unremitting attempts at genocide, culturalcide, and other forms of political and philosophical erasure. Native communities or nations have something the world needs to know about: the insight of continuity. We are here in Venice today because of the continuity of our local knowledge as culture, and often this is expressed as art. Michelson's *TwoRow II*, Belmore's *Fountain*, Luna's *Emendatio* are examples of those continuous points. *TwoRow II* remembers and reinterprets the meaning of an early contact point; it is compelling that this idea is still relevant today. The shift from wampum to a video projection enhances the concept. That is what artists do. It is the work of indigenous artists to make this work relevant to an international non-indigenous audience as well as a local audience. The conference and gathering are a first step in affirming our presence in the multivalent space of the local and the global.

Artist and curator Jolene Rickard (Tuscarora) is an associate professor at the State University of New York at Buffalo, where she holds a joint appointment in the departments of Art and Art History.

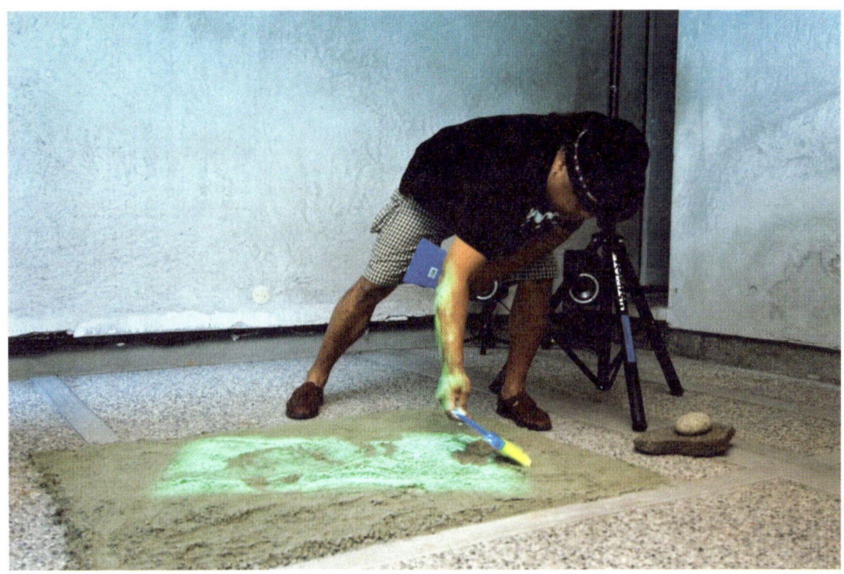

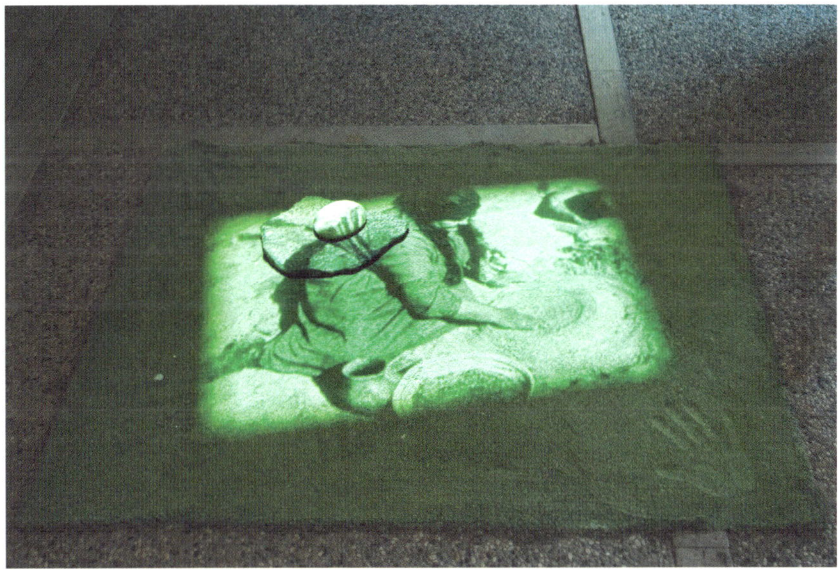

Artist James Luna (Luiseño) preparing "Apparitions: Past and Present," one of two installations for *Emendatio*, at the 2005 Venice Biennale. Photo by Katherine Fogden. © NMAI.

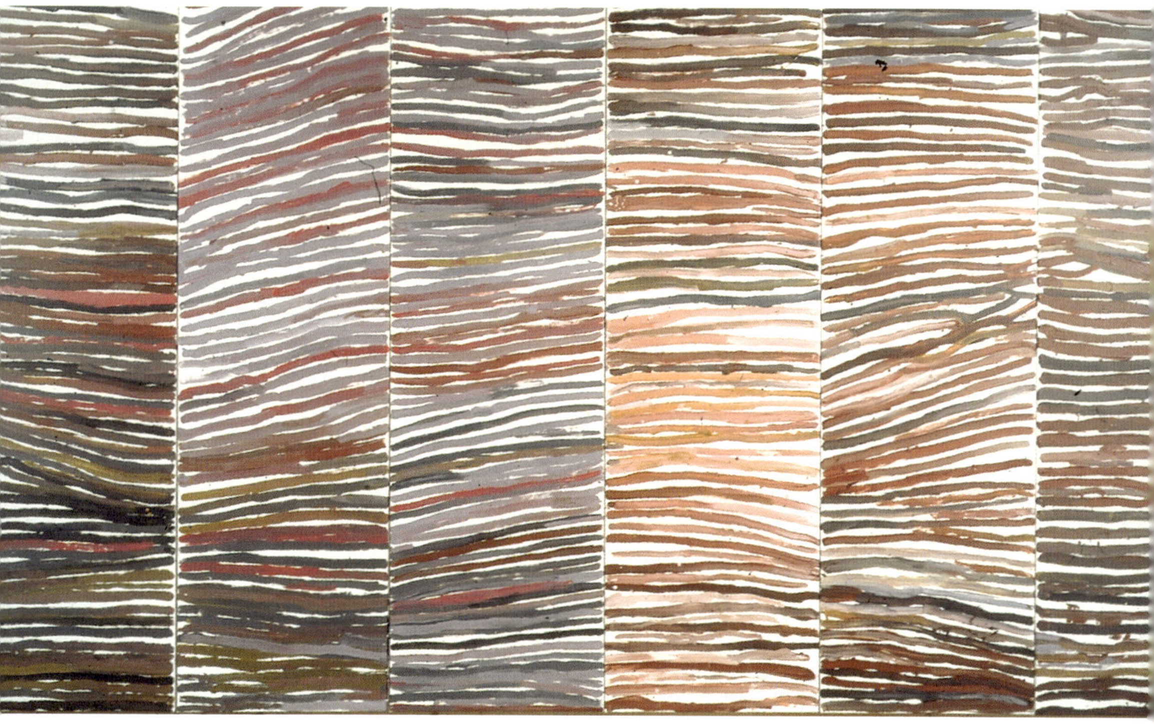

Emily Kame Kngwarreye (Anmatyerre, 1910–1996), *Untitled (Alweye)*, 1994. Synthetic polymer paint on canvas, six panels, 190 x 57 cm each. © 2006 Artists Rights Society (ARS), New York/VISCOPY, Australia. Photo © Brenda L. Croft.

BRENDA L. CROFT

Meeting, Not Colliding

I am an Aboriginal woman from the Gurindji/Mutpurra nations in the Northern Territory of Australia on my father's side—we are desert people. On my mother's side, I am Anglo-Australian, with German, Irish, and English heritage. In my country, however, if you identify as Aboriginal and are accepted as such by your people and the community in which you live, then that is that—no "part" this, no "percentage" that.

Indigenous people in Australia are two distinct groups: Aboriginal people, from mainland Australia and the Tiwi Islands off northern Australia, and Torres Strait Islander people, from the Torres Strait, in the region between Cape York of Far North Queensland and Papua New Guinea. Within these two groups are literally hundreds of distinct nations. In the 2001 national census, Aboriginal and Torres Strait Islander people comprised approximately two percent of Australia's total population, or around 400,000 people. In contrast to this small population percentage, indigenous people in Australia register in the highest percentages of negative indicators: infant mortality, poor health, shorter life expectancy, illiteracy, incarceration, unemployment, poor housing, low-level education, drug and alcohol abuse, and domestic violence rates. This is not news to any indigenous person from elsewhere in the world.

Before European contact, hundreds of nations existed within this continent, much in the same way as in the Americas. Although languages and customary practices have been adversely affected by two hundred years of colonization, we do not exist in isolation from one another. The majority of indigenous Australians—around seventy-five percent of our people—today live on the eastern seaboard, yet most non-indigenous Australian focus continues to be on Aboriginal people in other areas: central Australia, home to the "dot" painting movement; further north in tropical Arnhem Land, which contains some of the most striking rock art galleries in the world and bark painters of renown; or to the west in the Kimberley region of Western Australia, which was home to internationally acclaimed artists such as the late Rover Thomas (ca. 1926–1998). That is to say, the focus is on brown- and black-skinned people of the desert and bush/tropical "jungle." Greater numbers of indigenous people in Australia, however, live—as I do—in urban environs away from our people's traditional lands; yet we retain strong connections with our communities and cultural heritage. I thought it important to frame these facts so that you will grasp the realities, as opposed to the myths, regarding where indigenous Australians live, work, connect, and network.

I was an artist long before I was a curator. I grew up surrounded by mainly kitsch representations of Aboriginal art and culture: black velvet renditions of nubile, dusky, come-hither Aboriginal maidens or luscious, shiny-skinned, muscular Aboriginal men; tea towels, black "Mammy" dolls, placemats with poor reproductions of our first renowned and acknowledged Aboriginal artist, Albert Namatjira (1902–1959), an Arrernte man from Hermannsburg in central Australia; and books portraying indigenous culture as it was then considered: redundant, fractured beyond repair, and close to extinction. My Anglo-Australian mother wanted to ensure that my brothers and I were encouraged in and proud of our Aboriginal identity, even if the tools with which she was able to provide this were limited and problematic. My father, perhaps as an acknowledgment of his cultural dislocation, established a small Aboriginal arts and crafts/artifacts section in my parents' small business enterprise—a news agency located in a fairly narrow-minded country town in the early 1970s. I was always interested in visual arts, and this was supported by my parents in my childhood.

A stint at art school in the mid 1980s when I was in my early twenties was not a particularly successful time; although I received substantial support from senior lecturers, I also encountered ignorance from some tutors who challenged my Aboriginality and ridiculed my right to create work relating to my urban experiences as an indigenous woman living in Sydney. I was fortunate, however, to meet a group of Aboriginal artists, whose origins were all outside Sydney, many from interstate, who were also being subjected to incorrect notions about themselves and their art. As a collective, we established in late 1987 the first and only urban-based indigenous art center: Boomalli Aboriginal Artists Co-operative. As artists, our heritage was the foundation of our identity and could not be extricated from our art. In my case, I wanted to create images which reflected my existence in the increasingly politically and socially aware climate of the time.

Observations of a Curator and Artist

I became a curator by default, partly from wanting to organize the kind of exhibitions that I and other indigenous, urban-based and trained artists wanted to see. Hetti Perkins, Victoria Lynn, and I curated the Australian pavilion at the 47th Venice Biennale (1997); the exhibition was deliberately framed within a non-political, specifically contemporary art space. I curated the 2000 Adelaide Biennial of Australian Art, *Beyond the Pale: Contemporary Indigenous Art*, which was politically charged, unapologetically so. As an artist, I have been represented in a few of the 110 or so biennales/triennales that exist or did exist in the global art world at the end of the twentieth century: the 9th Biennale of Sydney, *The Boundary Rider,* in 1992; the inaugural Johannesburg Biennale, *Africus,* in 1995; the sole Melbourne International Biennial, *Signs of Life*; and the *al latere* section of the 48th Venice Biennale in *Oltre il mito (Beyond myth)* (1999). For the most part, these experiences only served to increase my desire to generate exhibitions outside existing, mainstream circuits. I do not wish to sound ungrateful, but we are constantly being forced into the role of the *exotic* or *primitive*, nearly two decades after *Magiciens de la terre*, held in 1989 at the Pompidou Center in Paris.

To explain, I will b(l)acktrack a bit. I was working as an Aboriginal artist in Sydney in the 1980s—the decade of the high-profile *Magiciens* exhibition, which served to reinforce in many ways the idea of the noble/ancient/mystical/creator, with the artists, pure and untouched, presented with their work like holy relics. Given this construct, urban Aboriginal artists from Australia—often considered "half-castes" or "half-white"—were even more invisible than our countrymen and women living in the desert, the bush, or the tropics. If an Aboriginal artist's work did not look like that which was displayed in exhibitions such as *Magiciens,* and he or she did not resemble the artists accompanying their work in these exhibitions, there was little chance of being taken seriously—certainly not if the work was in media other than the accepted "traditional," i.e., bark paintings in ochre or dot-style paintings in acrylic.

This changed in the late 1980s with the advent of a number of artists who happened to be of Aboriginal heritage—Tracy Moffatt (one of Boomalli's founding members) and Gordon Bennett among the most notable. Aligning themselves with the postmodernist construct, however, these two artists emphatically positioned themselves as contemporary artists only and refuted any reading of or engagement with their work as "Aboriginal art." Their position was that they wanted their work to be considered alongside their nonindigenous contemporaries. To be both would perhaps be having one's cake and eating it, too. The problem was that this served to place, or displace, the artist in limbo—non-person's land. It is ironical that while Paris, the "heart" of Europe and high Western culture, was presenting in *Magiciens* a reinforcement of colonial voyeurism under the veil of postcolonial paradigm, a revolution was taking place in the antipodes among indigenous cultural activists in the world's "youngest" country (a title given to Australia by non-indigenous powers).

By the time of the inaugural Johannesburg Biennale, *Africus,* in 1995, I was a bit savvier, and found myself concerned at the seeming pointlessness of much of the event. Staying in a five-star hotel, guarded by local uniformed personnel wielding semi-automatic weapons, I felt as if I were on a dangerous Club Med tour for select(ed) artists. The disengagement with the local community was painfully clear as construction tools, equipment, and artworks vanished. Who could blame people so poor for helping themselves to the excess of materials laid out so temptingly, as if to rub their noses in what they lacked? It was also my first awakening to how peripheral artists could be to an event; *Africus* was very much about the curators' network, not about acknowledgment of the participating artists.

The international conglomerate, The Rolling Stones, was conducting its first tour of South Africa while we were at the biennale, and our sightings of other celebrities such as David Bowie and his wife, model and author Iman, strolling through the exhibition only added to the surreality of the situation. Poverty was endemic, and although the event took place in the heady days following the end of apartheid—with the main venue, formerly the Afrikana Museum, renamed Museum Afrika as a tilt towards re-writing/righting the history of the country—tension permeated the atmosphere. The J'burg Biennale was too ambitious to last, and its next staging was its death knell. Held in a country just emerging as an undeveloped chrysalis from its restrictive political cocoon, this overloaded event was too top-heavy in its misdirected aims, and the organizers' "melting pot" thesis quickly degenerated into a morass of "could have been" scenarios.

Looking to the Future

Many other biennales/triennales could be discussed in relation to the multiple issues raised in our session, but there is not time for that, so I will briefly address two final points. First, in relation to the establishment of culture- and gender-specific institutions and exhibitions, I worked on the Australian Indigenous Art Commission (AIAC) for the new Musée du Quai Branly in Paris. Although indigenous objects and art from Australia are a very small component of the collection—only 1,600 out of nearly 400,000 objects—the architectural team headed by the internationally renowned Jean Nouvel specified from the beginning that their plan for the building would include contemporary indigenous art from Australia.

When I and AIAC co-curator Hetti Perkins were approached by the Australian government to submit a proposal, we emphasized that we were determined not to follow previous ephemeral representations, such as sand sculptures à la *Magiciens,* in which the artists were on display as much as their work. The commission is such that if the Musée powers wish to remove the works at some future point, they will have to demolish the building in which the artworks are sited; to paraphrase one of the artists involved, Judy Watson, you could say we have attempted to colonize the building and the institution.

My last point is to draw attention to Geeta Kapur's presentation earlier this week at the Storr symposium—for me, certainly one of the most pertinent of the entire week. More's the pity that it was so abruptly truncated for reasons of time, depriving us of the opportunity to hear her conclusion or engage in discussion about it. Geeta's paper was the only one that challenged the existing status quo of juggernaut biennales that mainly continue to reflect and reference each other, overseen by an international curatorial club that allows little room for inclusion or engagement for/by people of color or those outside the existing trade routes.

I especially welcomed Geeta's comments regarding the establishment of further biennales, as I am working with my employing institution, the National Gallery of Australia, to initiate a National Contemporary Indigenous Triennale, which is due to have its inception in late 2007. The most important lesson I gleaned from attending the symposium is that we need to push forward with such ideas and create our own spaces as it seems unlikely that we will be allowed to play with the big boys. I am less interested in knocking on doors, asking, "Please sir, may I have some more?" than I am in working in the region where I live with like-minded curators and artists. Start in the antipodes, Australia at first, and then expand to include the surrounding international regions and address that which was overlooked by the Bienal de Habana—the various axes of the Southern Hemisphere.

Only certain privileged art worlds gathered during the past few days, but in the future we hope that more worlds—and more diverse ones—will be welcomed and will truly meet at a multiplicity of centers, rather than merely colliding.

Brenda L. Croft (Gurindji/Mutpurra), Senior Curator of Aboriginal and Torres Strait Islander Art at the National Gallery of Australia in Canberra, is also an artist.

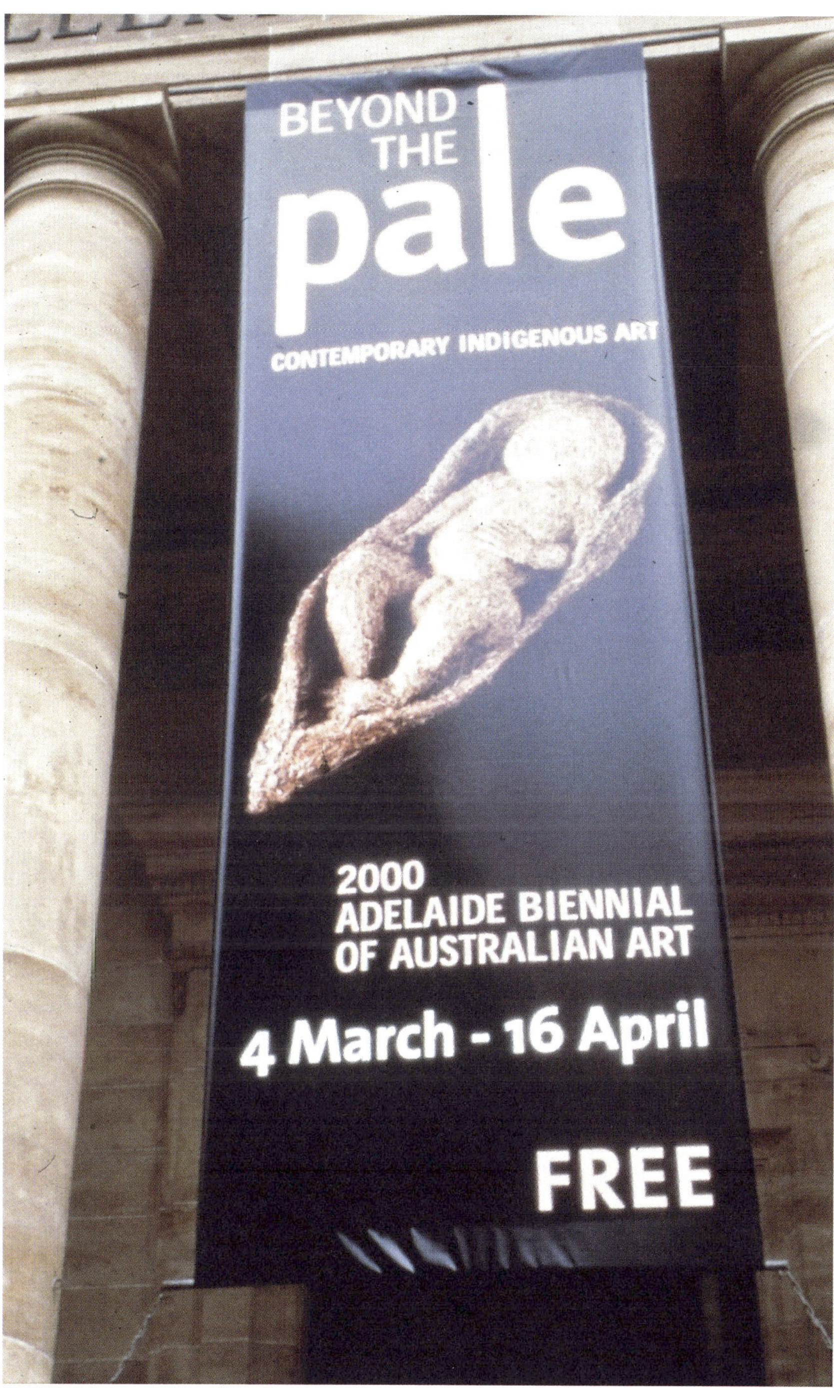

An image of *Baby* (1999) by Nyoongar artist Joyce Winsley (1938–2001) appears on this banner for *Beyond the Pale: Contemporary Indigenous Art*, 2000 Adelaide Biennial of Australian Art. Photo © Brenda L. Croft.

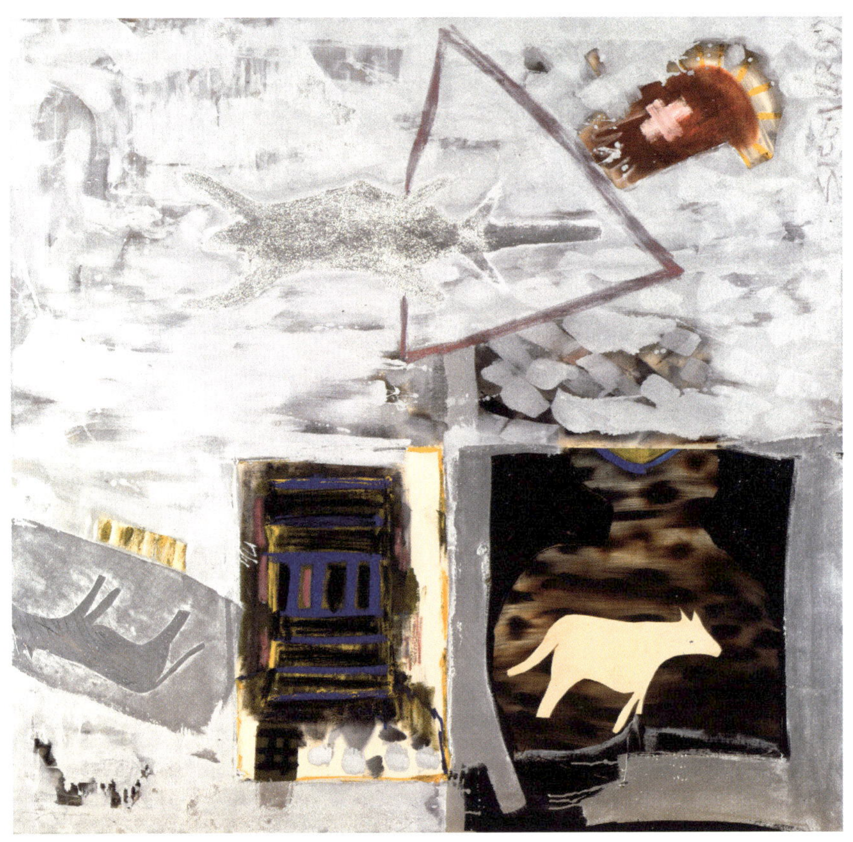

Siron Franco (Brazilian, b. 1947), *Memória/Memory*, 1990–92. Mixed media on canvas, 180 x 191 cm. Donated by Charles Cosac, UECLAA #1. © University of Essex Collection of Latin American Art.

IVO MESQUITA

A Latin American Perspective

I would like to begin with a memory of a dear and profound experience from my residency period in Canada in 1988 as a visiting curator at the Winnipeg Art Gallery. As part of this six-month residency, I had the gratifying opportunity to travel throughout the country; to become acquainted with its museums, galleries, and professionals; and to visit the studios of a considerable number of artists. At the end of my stay, I was interviewed by *The Winnipeg Free Press* newspaper about my Canadian sojourn. I said that among several challenging and transforming experiences the most notable had been my contact with a very specific theme being debated within the country's artistic community: the demand for the right of Native Canadian artists and curators to have their work exhibited and represented alongside that of other Canadians at the National Gallery of Canada rather than only at the Canadian Museum of Civilization, both in Ottawa. (I met Gerald McMaster, one of the proponents of that debate and one of its most eloquent voices, during this time.) This discussion was a revelation for me, something that seemed unique, civilized, democratic, and extremely stimulating. My understanding of my own situation as a curator coming from Latin America—a region where the "First Nations people" did not have any political or artistic visibility—was transformed.

Today in Venice, as I think about that debate, I remember that for a significant number of people it meant crossing over a river that divided the city of Ottawa and separated the two museums. Now, seventeen years later, the issue has crossed the Atlantic Ocean and installed itself in this Italian palace, to be discussed within a much broader perspective and an international context. This fact represents an achievement and advance in the quality of the inclusion and visibility of Native American artists and augurs well for this conference.

I bring a Brazilian and Latin American perspective to the issues we are addressing, and I present some points about strategic planning to include contemporary Native artistic productions and practices into an evermore interdependent and globalized circuit. I also delineate certain ideas that I believe are undervalued within the contemporary artistic debate.

My first point refers to the notion of "art" and the role that it played in the political, social, and cultural establishment of Latin America. One could say that the process that today we call globalization began in Latin America. In reality, by the mid sixteenth century globalization had already arrived in Japan with the Portuguese fleet. Through trade and commerce with the indigenous inhabitants and until the expulsion of the religious Christians a century later, this contact brought to Japan among other things more than two hundred words that are still in use today. It is important to comprehend the colonization process as a process of Westernization through the propagation of capitalism and Christianity among the conquered peoples. As such, the colonizer appealed to three principal strategies: commerce, religion, and art.

The colonial project of bringing newly discovered lands into the means, styles, and values of Western civilization began under the regency of the Baroque, the first international style, which flourished well beyond European frontiers through local interpretations and colors in diverse latitudes of the planet such as the Philippines, India, and Western Africa. In Latin America, it also obtained the contours of a "mestizo" language of forms, discourse, and representation, establishing the foundations of architecture, music, literature, and art on the continent and, more important, defining a way of thinking, conforming itself to the local sensibilities—the basis for the work of various artists until the contemporary current.[1] Whatever existed before the arrival of the colonizer was destroyed, pillaged, expropriated, and acculturated. The survivors were excluded, confined, and tutored on reservations or on the periphery of the economy of their various countries. (Resistance still bravely lives on in Chiapas in Mexico or with the *cocaleros* in Bolivia, Peru, Ecuador, and Colombia—certainly, though, a museum or biennial is not a priority in those areas). Their histories, traditions, and monuments are exploited by the tourist industry, however, without payment of their due royalties.

In the beginning of the nineteenth century, when the Latin American colonies began to obtain their independence and create modern states, the nations on the continent were founded within the ideals of the Enlightenment, the French Revolution, and North American democracy. Thus, Western values and parameters were articulated within a system based on Western institutions such as the judicial system, parliament, education, and the museum. New national images were created, but, at the same time, the choice of socio-political model was already indicative of the level of Westernization in which these burgeoning republics functioned.[2] Latin American countries have almost two hundred years of republican history, and thus postcolonial theories, generally speaking, are not applicable here as the colonial past is a part of the collective memory, elaborated, systematized by local writing of history, and unfolding itself into our present reality.

Negotiating Art

From these small and brief glimpses into history, we note that choices were made and decisions taken, for better or worse, and we can infer that we have been responsible for them, in a large or small degree, in ways that were more or less just and democratic. In the same manner, we are also responsible for our "self-colonizing" or "uncolonizing" today. In Latin America, we are always bringing pieces together, collecting fragments, and melding races, many histories, and diversified cultural experiences. We try to bestow density upon them, establishing foundations and pointing out relevancy to that which we consider ours. The important thing is to be clear that when we speak about art, we are speaking about the level of "Occidentalization" to which we are submitted or to which context we believe we belong. At a recent conference of the International Committee for Museums and Collections of Modern Art (CIMAM) in São Paulo, the historian Walter Mignolo, one of whose concerns is the relation between modernity and minority cultures, pointed out a very important difference between cultures and knowledge. For him, culture assumes something spontaneously generated while knowledge reveals a determination, desire, and rationality in its implementation. For him, art, museums, and biennials belong to a category (discipline and practice) related to an Occidental tradition of thinking and approximation to reality, working within concepts and parameters precisely defined and systematized.

Thus, the visibility of Latin American art today has to be negotiated in all instances that require its presence. It does not exist as an autonomous category of artistic practice and needs to be reinvented each time we wish to refer to it. It cannot be considered based on the fact that we are racially different, but rather because through it we express our consciousness of participating in a discipline and a territory with which we have deep links and where we find the significance of belonging.

My second point addresses the experience of Latin America with miscegenation of races and cultures. I think that the unique character of our contribution to Occidental culture and to the processes of globalization resides in the fact that we are mestizos and opposed to the hybrid notion so much in use today in texts and discussions about art and contemporary culture. A hybrid product supposes something generated in a laboratory, planned and developed under scientific conditions and control, such as seeds, flowers, fruits, or genes. The mestizo, on the contrary, is a product of an encounter, a shock, a friction—a confrontation of primary pulses, of desire, love, and hate. We are the New World, where the colonizer expatriated the Natives to establish and populate the continent with *criollos*, the term coined by the Spaniards to designate all who came from the colonies, independent of race, color, or culture. It is no accident that in the beginning of the eighteenth century the Spanish court decided to map the races that were being formed in its colonies in the Americas, seeking to identify and name the diverse miscegenation that was being formed there and that was, in its view, corrupting the European races.[3]

Also within this spirit and consciousness of mestizo development, one can note the work of the Martinique poet and activist Aimé Césaire, a founder of the Creole movement, with its strong influence on the postcolonial theories of Franz Fanon and the field of cultural studies. Despite the radical nature of his criticism of the French colonial system, Césaire never clamored for the independence of his island. On the contrary, he always asked for its autonomy and representation as a French province in the Americas. In the same manner, he championed in his writing not only the traditions and transformations of the language and culture brought by his African ancestors but also its fusion with the tradition of great French literature. He understood his work as a continuum, an unfolding of that history, which needs to be taken in the context of a process initiated with the colonization that changed the order of things in the name of God and commerce. What he seems to say is that to avoid manicheisms, resentments, and culpability, the important thing is to continue the debate, the possibility of criticism, and movement in the field.

In conclusion, I would like to respond to the question of whether or not to have separate museums for non-Western art. As I said earlier, if the theme is art, it refers to Occidental culture and ways of thinking. For us to be able to think about and define strategies for the visibility of minorities, we must consider the traditional art museum and how to approach it. I understand museums such as the National Museum of the American Indian or the National Museum of Women in the Arts as monuments to the struggles and efforts of these social and cultural groups toward inclusion and visibility. We need to be careful, however, to avoid converting these institutions into ghettos where these groups exist and present themselves. The critical element for the success of such institutions is the ability to extract strength from the productions housed therein, but at the same time to show flexibility, as if constituted of porous terrain and open to other influences. A museum of Latin American art is a fine idea, for instance, because a good volume of artistic production, qualified critical thought, and a history are all there to draw upon. The problem arises when contemporary artists turn these museums into ideological trenches, instead of seeking new spaces for confrontation, shock, or friction. Being in the world, subjected to the turbulences of life, seems to me the necessary condition of being an artist as well as a curator.

Ivo Mesquita is an independent curator in São Paulo, Brazil. The former director of the São Paulo Biennale and Museu de Arte Moderna, São Paulo, Mesquita has curated numerous exhibitions addressing the theme of cultural identity in Latin American art.

NOTES

1. In dealing with the cultural miscegenation that occurred in Latin America and the use of images in the propagation of faith, it is worth remembering as an example that in the task of Christianizing the pagans, the religious factions were forced to change European Christian iconography. The creation of the world could not be explained with the masculine figures of the Holy Trinity alone because the presence of a feminine figure able to give birth to the God child was fundamental to the Natives' understanding of creation. Hence, the presence of the Virgin at the center of the Trinity in many representations of the colonial period, as well as in the predominance of today's cult to her, mother of all in the continent, seen and adored as Our Lady of Guadalupe, of Copacabana, of Aparecida, of Luján, of Macarena, among so many others. In the same manner, the iconography of *arcabuzeiro* (musqueteer) angels are a concession to the Natives: how could the armies of God, the angels, be so powerful without the use of weapons? After all, how was it possible to dominate something without weapons? This is how they were subjugated. The new God that was taught them dominated everything, but could not do so without well-equipped armies.

2. It is worth noting that (a) as an exception to the other countries, Brazil, despite its independence from Portugal, continued for sixty-seven years as a kingdom under the regency of the princes of Orleans and Braganca; and (b) the frontiers of the Latin American countries, defined at the time of their independence, have experienced very few alterations or change since then.

3. Within the registries of this ethnic cartography are the famous "Paintings of Castes" that document and illustrate the races as they were formed in Hispanic America.

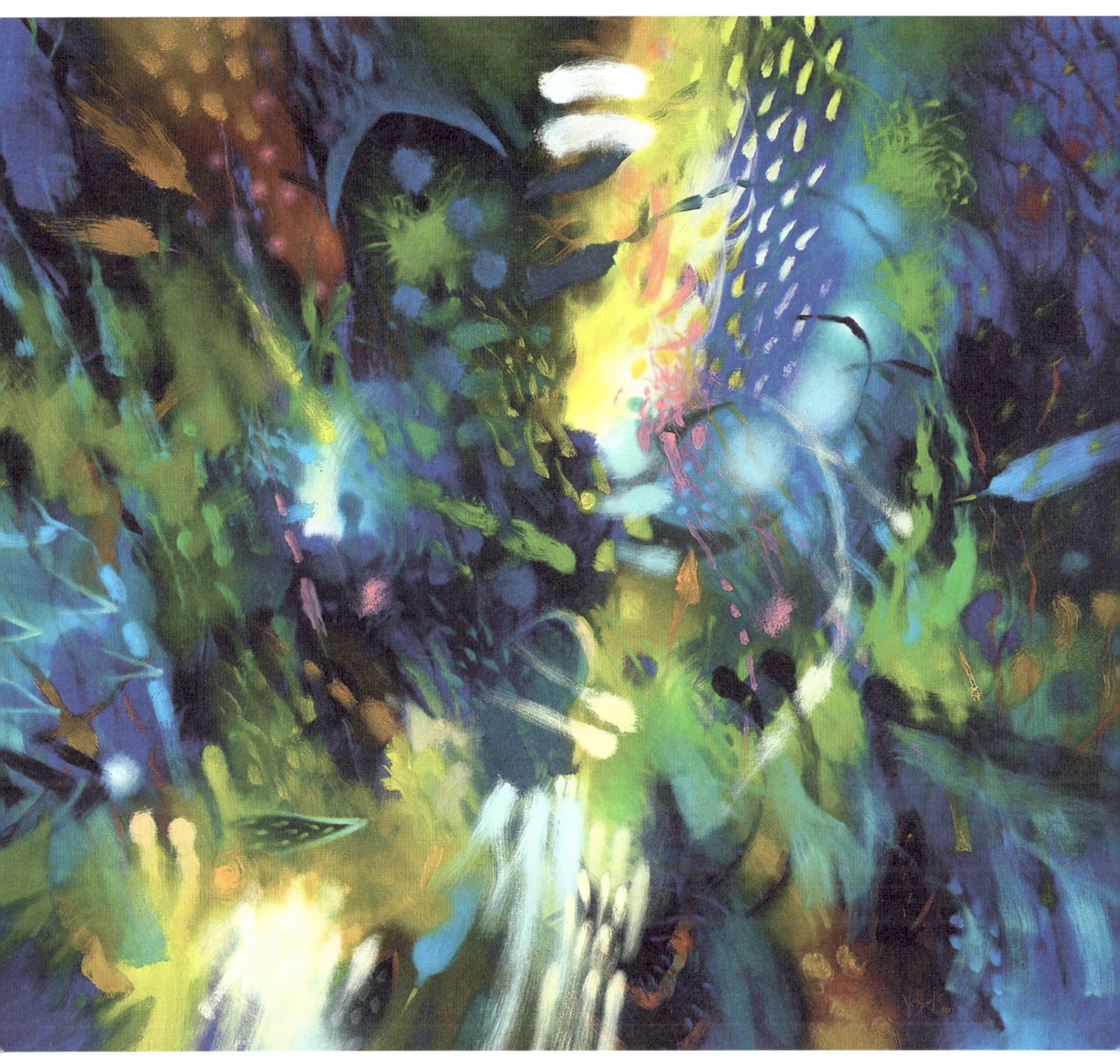

Carlos Jacanamijoy Tisoy (Inga Quichua, b. 1964), *A Rose in Tribute*, 2003. Oil on canvas, 170 x 140 cm. Collection of the National Museum of the American Indian (26/1565). Photo by Walter Larrimore. © NMAI.

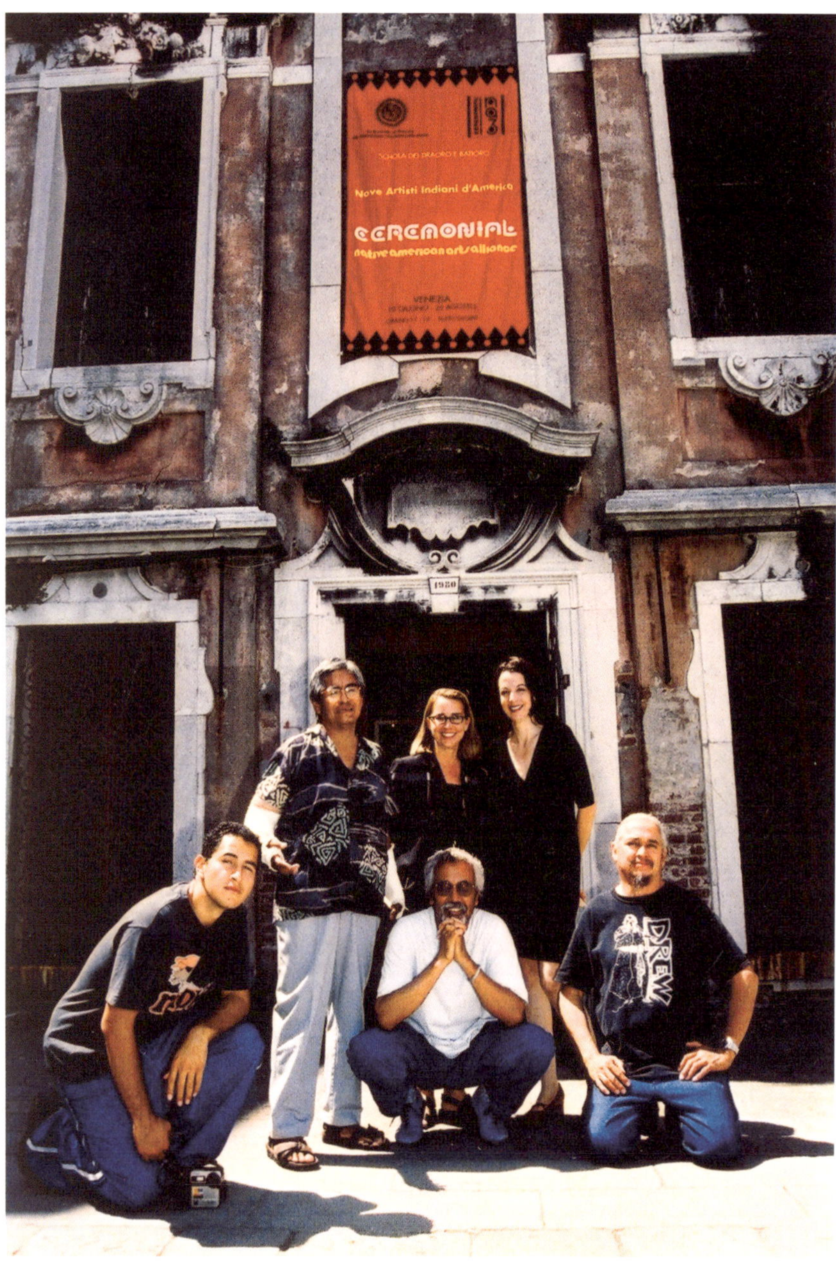

Native American Arts Alliance (NA3) team members in front of the Schola dei Tiraoro e Battioro, the venue for *Ceremonial* at the 1999 Venice Biennale, June 10, 1999. Standing (left to right): Simon Ortiz, Patsy Phillips, Nancy Marie Mithlo. Seated (left to right): Gabriel Lopez Shaw, Harry Fonseca, Bob Haozous. Photo by Mario di Martino. Courtesy of Department of Special Collections, Stanford University Libraries.

NANCY MARIE MITHLO

"Give, Give, Giving": Cultural Translations

This essay is dedicated to my friend and mentor Harry Fonseca.
His enthusiasm for the beauty of life continues to inspire us.

When asked to evaluate my curatorial work recently, an academic colleague exclaimed, "Three exhibits at the Venice Biennale is a big deal!" I thought it was a big deal, too, not necessarily for myself alone, but for the talented artists and educators who have joined me there over the past decade. Making one's way into the Biennale requires commitment to one's craft, phenomenal networking skills, and the ever-elusive combination of talent and capital. An artist, an organization, or a curator does not come by chance to participate in this grand manifestation of all things current in the arts. To develop an understanding of the complexities of the Venice Biennale as a phenomenon takes years, perhaps a lifetime; to become an actor within this living, breathing, endlessly changing global conversation takes effort. Sometimes it takes a lot of effort.

The 1999 Venice Biennale exhibition *Ceremonial,* sponsored by the Native American Arts Alliance (NA3), a Santa Fe, New Mexico-based organization that I helped found, was designed to commemorate the incorporation of Native American voices into the artistic dialogues of the Biennale. By invoking the concept of ceremony, this group of educators, artists, and activists referenced the concept of public witnessing for central life events.

Just as one cannot be properly named, married, or buried without the participation of a larger community, NA3 sought recognition as a participant within the structure of the international arts community. Against enormous organizational and financial constraints, this collective—later renamed the Indigenous Arts Action Alliance (IA3)—exhibited Native art at the Venice Biennale three times (in 1999, 2001, and 2003) before bequeathing the project to the Smithsonian's National Museum of the American Indian for their 2005 exhibit at the Biennale.[1] Our collective work over the years naturally led to the expectation that something significant might come out of this participation; that the beauty and wisdom of a Native aesthetic might finally be recognized if Native Americans themselves were the ones speaking.

This hope for an immediate recognition by established arts journals and critics was largely unfulfilled. The resounding silence from magazines, fine arts museums, and our professional peers (Native and non-Native) following *Ceremonial* was characterized by NA3 board member and artist Harry Fonseca in terms of ripples. Instead of a growing, influential reaction—like a pebble tossed into a lake with concentric circles radiating outward—he observed that the public response was more akin to a rock dropped into a vat of frybread oil—no "blip" with expanding ripples, but a solid "bloop" to the bottom of the kettle (sound effects help with this particular telling).[2] James Luna's comment that "my phone isn't exactly ringing off the hook" after the 2005 Biennale exhibit *Emendatio* reflects a similar realization.[3] We have witnessed a decade of Native arts exhibitions at the Biennale, yet Native arts have yet to be treated seriously. By seriously, I mean more than a token mention of the exotic Native in mainstream contemporary arts curricula, publications, or exhibitions. The apparent indifference to Native arts suggests exhibition alone is insufficient. Meaningful appraisals that incorporate alternative artistic worlds—what Robert Storr, curator of the 2007 Venice Biennale, takes pains to reference as multiple "sites of art"—are needed."[4]

Other Desires, Other Agendas

Yet this articulation of sovereign intellectual standing is often obscured by other desires, other agendas. The curatorial philosophy of arts scholar and fellow Biennale curator Salah Hassan is illustrative of the twin tensions that seem inseparable in a platform that seeks inclusion: a perceived assimilation to standard art canons, countered by the claim to cultural specificity. In other words, how can we achieve what one NA3 board member termed "the get in" while also retaining a sense of our genuineness, without bending so far as to lose a sense of self. Is it possible that the "get in" philosophy is ultimately a disservice to cultural integrity? Hassan's declaration, "If you do not exhibit, you do not exist!" has become something of a rallying cry for artists newly entering from the fringes.[5] The well-received 2001 Biennale show curated by Hassan, *Authentic/Ex-Centric: Africa in and out of Africa* was, in his words, "an effort to remedy the virtual absence of Africa in the Venice Biennale."[6] Hassan's call for visibility, however, is complicated by the simultaneous desire for acknowledgment; in this case, acknowledgment of African artists as important contributors to Western artistic movements such as conceptualism, the theme of the show. Hassan argues that the legitimization of African conceptual artists hinges on the practice of exhibitions. As Hassan explains, "Exhibitions remain exemplar of how art history is produced."[7] Conversely, I have come to conclude that exhibitions alone are insufficient. The "get in" is a hollow goal in the absence of a grounded cultural understanding. Visibility alone is really only another form of voyeurism. Indian people have been subjected to the incessant gaze of the West since Contact. It is not enough to be looked upon, serving as the exotic other in an exchange that has profound negative implications for self-representation. Scholars Lutz and Collins refer to this imbalanced power dynamic as a "culturally tutored experience" that presents as natural that which is really ahistorical, patriarchal, and constructed.[8] To see fully is to be able to translate aesthetic conventions cross-culturally. The mimicking of Western terminology is a form of colonialism, an assimilation to Western constructs and norms.

I believe Hassan's position is ultimately more complex and nuanced than the inclusive battle cry suggests. For example, his essay in the exhibition catalogue for *Authentic/Ex-Centric* calls for "reciprocal traffic of influences between Africa and the rest of the world" as well as recognition of an "African standpoint."[9] Yet these more subtle sentiments are masked by the dictation that exhibitions serve as the essential component of minority arts activism. This aphorism is especially problematic when transferred to the realm of Native American arts. "If you do not exhibit, you do not exist"—how can this possibly be so in Native American contexts? After surviving centuries of genocidal oppression, could we really be rendered nonexistent merely by being left out of critical arts dialogues? Clearly, this mandate cannot reflect Native sensibilities. This is the soul-searching moment, the necessary departure—the point at which we might abandon the hope of inclusion for inclusion's sake alone.

A Proactive Frame of Reference

The purpose of contemporary Native arts criticism in a more proactive frame of reference is less about what others think (getting in and being witnessed by others as in a ceremony) and more about what we think of ourselves in relationship with others. Contemporary Native arts criticism then offers a parallel conception of aesthetic discourse. This worldview serves as a meaningful alternative to the assimilationist desire to be recognized by mainstream art conventions. This alternative conceptual approach is a more challenging, circuitous method; it calls for a double vision of the type that intellectual and civil rights activist W. E. B. DuBois termed the third eye or double consciousness.[10] In DuBois's words, "the Negro is a sort of seventh son, born with a veil, and gifted with second-sight in this American world.[11] DuBois offers potent application for Native arts criticism, for while the world may yield no favors for the recognition of a Native aesthetic, this aesthetic is available nonetheless. Despite a lack of mainstream institutional recognition, a multiplicity of artistic dialects and worldviews exist. In this frame of reference—one not dependent on art historical canons—cultural translations are necessary for a global arts conversation to ensue. A sovereign, culturally specific platform that is simultaneously engaged with larger art currents can emerge if space is made available outside of the standardized inclusion/legitimization agenda.

The established platform of the international art exhibition enables the multiple translations I am seeking. In a world where Native people continue to be colonized economically, culturally, and politically, we do not have the luxury of ignoring the mainstream. But acceptance in global venues is only one step; acceptance of one's own artistic orientation is the more central goal. For Native people, these unique aesthetic traditions include cultural imperatives that reward service, sharing, and community responsibility as well as an active embrace of contemporaneous influences. What I am calling for is not a separate playing field, not a replication of the ethnic arts segmentation that often results in stagnation, but rather recognition of the cultural translations necessary for true parity in the global arts arena. Remarkably, the Venice Biennale accommodates these interventions without restrictive control.

Repositioning the conversation away from the perception of inclusion or exclusion in mainstream dialogues toward recognition of alternative knowledge systems at play demands that convergences and chasms among various art systems be directly addressed. Indigenous communities can creatively deconstruct the notion of curatorial authority that has come to define what serious players in the arts arena do, especially in the global arena. Multiple conceptions of leadership and shared leadership, rather than self-defined curatorial power, constitute the major defining characteristic of this curatorial direction. The NA3 organization's planning process utilized diffuse and, at times, consensual decision-making processes. When the 1999 team, for example, was forced to hang Jaune Quick-to-See Smith's fiber installation piece *Shot Heard Round the World* in a space a fraction of the size for which it was intended, five individuals debated the most appropriate action. It ultimately fell to the two professional artists, Harry Fonseca and Bob Haozous, to make the final call, given their training and experience. When dealing with this and other quandaries, no sole curatorial authority prevailed.

It appears that the Venice Biennale may be developing along similar decentralized lines of inquiry. Davide Croff, president of La Biennale di Venezia, stated at the 2005 Storr symposium *Where Art Worlds Meet: Multiple Modernities and the Global Salon* that the Biennale "cannot ask that the curator be the sole and exclusive interpreter of the Institution's entire project."[12] Yet other opinions on the topic exist simultaneously. Speaking at the same symposium, Carlos Basualdo, an Argentinean poet, critic, and curator living in the United States, argued that large-scale exhibits demand an element of interpretation for a growing public. He further suggested that it falls to the role of the curator to include this discursive component as a structural necessity.[13] Native artists and curators have relevant contributions to make to this debate, contributions that can enrich the narrow theoretical options currently available. Parity, consensual decision-making, and complementarity are all potent and useful organizational strategies that can be mobilized within the existing structure of the international art exhibition.

What makes Native-run international exhibits unique? Native efforts have the added dimension of a concerted non-individualistic orientation. Each of NA3/IA3's Biennale exhibits had a component of mentorship enacted as a central premise of the exhibit process. The 2003 exhibit *Pellerossasogna* featured the work of Mohawk filmmaker Shelley Niro and Diné poet Sherwin Bitsui. While Niro was a seasoned artist with an international reputation, Bitsui was an emerging artist just entering the global arena. Organizers of the exhibit saw it as a unique opportunity to have these artists exhibit together, complementing each other's work. Small things counted, such as Shelley's immense calm when the film projector malfunctioned or how Sherwin captivated visitors at the opening with an impassioned reading of his work. Among my favorite memories of that hot, hot summer were the times when Shelley would turn and ask offhandedly, "Are you hungry, Sherwin?" We would duck into a cool cafe for tiny, soft Italian sandwiches and cappuccino, oblivious of the time. I do not think we have the language to adequately describe the importance of these tender nuances. I can only say that there was no star, and we looked after one another. Experience counted, yes, but just as important was the respect accorded to each person's contributions to the whole, as well as one's limitations.

A Twofold Task

The task of interpreting this alternative Native curatorial methodology is twofold: existing interpretative tools must be mentally dismantled and more satisfactory concepts identified and articulated. Collective curatorial author-

ity is actually more difficult and demanding than the sole authority definition of the role. This is not a matter of novice work, flawed vision, or a lack
of professionalism, but rather a concerted effort to have the process of exhibiting art find congruence with other tribal norms. That we would choose
to follow this methodology at the Biennale was so foreign as to be unthink-
able to most reviewers and even potential exhibiting artists. Harried jour-
nalists often arrived at the 2001 exhibit *Umbilicus* demanding object lists
with artists' names. When I explained that the installations were collectively
designed and built by a team of artists, the condescension was palpable.
Surely, their dismissal seemed to imply, we were amateurs!

Likewise, Native artists invited to exhibit under the NA3/IA3 collective
enterprises often declined to participate once they understood that the organizers did not intend to supervise their financial and organizational needs, but
rather expected the artists to raise their own travel, shipping, and subsistence
monies as well as choose the art they intended to exhibit. The passivity (and
often victimization) of the chosen artist role becomes glaringly apparent once
these support structures and established art curatorial practices are dismantled. When asked to participate equally in the work of mounting an international exhibition, many artists declined, having become accustomed to the in-
dividualism and non-participation of established art curatorial practices.

In addition to the task of conveying our curatorial methodology to others, we face the difficulty of translating contemporary Native identity. Here
I would like to quote from one of the few assessments of the 1999 exhibit
Ceremonial—an article in the *International Herald Tribune* by Roderick Conway
Morris. Morris sensitively tried to convey our perceived plight: while suc-
cessfully "avoiding the folkloric," neither did we achieve full fluidity in the
language of the postmodern, which appeared to be "alien." The resulting
"dissonance" was evidently a "search for an idiom to satisfy both tradition
and life in today's world." The exhibit's worth was attributed to its "poignant"
and "thought-producing" qualities.[14] This exiled space—neither a prisoner
to culture nor a hybridized, cosmopolitan individual—is one to which the
contemporary Native artist seems endlessly condemned. We failed to achieve
parity as postmodern participants, but we were deemed interesting in our

attempts all the same. A fundamental break in understanding occurs when only select conceptual categories are at play—postmodern, conceptual, and traditional. Recognition of cultural specificity is essential at this juncture.

The contemporary Native American art field has not reached a point at which it can effectively position the visual culture of Native North America as a component of indigenous knowledge systems in tandem with similar developments in economic, ecological, or political spheres. Indigenous knowledge (often referred to by the acronym "IK") is understood to reference the wisdom of Native approaches to agriculture, hunting, environmental management, or sovereignty efforts in legal realms. IK has not, however, developed along similar paths in the aesthetic world of global fine arts. This is not to say that Native people have never understood the broader ramifications of the visual as an integral part of a philosophical worldview, but rather that we have become distracted from this internal and processual orientation, which could offer a useful theoretical structure for aesthetic analysis. Instead of attempting to codify this still-emerging aesthetic, it may be more productive to define the contours of an indigenous orientation by what it is not. The Native American experience does not lend itself easily to standard artistic paradigms. Modernism, dialectics, and parody have been key concepts in the reception of contemporary Native American arts. These approaches, however, distract rather than clarify; they present Native aesthetic philosophers with a reactive rather than a proactive orientation.

The postmodern has a long history of being falsely applied to Native arts constructs. The failure of this point of reference to encompass indigenous ideologies is in no small part due to the immense difficulty of codifying an approach to knowledge that is fluid and often diffuse. The authors of "Globalisation and Indigenous Peoples: Threat or Empowerment?" argue that the Western tradition of education grounded in written traditions contributes to this problem. They provocatively ask, "Is it possible to present the fluid and multivalent characteristics of Indigenous systems of knowledge in an authentic manner, one that is not canonical but that is open to subtle formulations that are part of practice and traditional cultural values?"[15] Equally problematic is the frequency with which the intent of Native artists is misread. The artists featured in *Ceremonial* were not striving for an idiom to express the tensions between tradition and life in today's world as the *International Herald Tribune* reviewer suggested; they were expressing life in today's world. The binary of tradition and modernism—construed as our enduring "struggle"—constitutes a major obstacle to recognizing the multiple "sites of art" the Storr symposium advocates.

My critique follows a line of inquiry similar to the one historian Philip J. Deloria advanced about modernity in his 2004 book *Indians in Unexpected Places*.[16] Deloria argues that Indians have been denied modernity because of their utilization as carriers of authenticity and primitivism. Indian people, he concludes, helped to create modernity in dialogue with others by being cast as actors in representational moments that juxtaposed primitivism and modernity. By virtue of this role in the ideological discourse of the West, Native Americans serve as a "functional narrative" for the anxieties of modernism. Indians function as an inverted norm, the underside of modernist realities. Viewed in this light, Native bodies are only shadows to the real work of modernism happening in the arts as well as politics. Any hesitancy to work for what our *International Herald Tribune* commentator described as "the worldwide postmodernist gallery and curatorial establishment," situates the Native as not simply exiled from participating in the mainstream but also as unwilling or unable to participate. Reliance upon an inclusion/exclusion orientation results in only two role options—reluctant primitives or angry Indians. Both approaches lead to tiring and ultimately uninteresting results.

Without recognition of these larger metanarratives at play, arts conversations in the vein of the popular hybrid, globalized norm can appear to be libratory and progressive but in fact be reifying. The anxieties of the postmodern West are served by a dialectical conversation with the non-West. Viewed as indicators of the ground, how can Native arts constructs possibly be read correctly as critical arts appraisals, as positive form rather than negative outline? In *The Third Eye: Race, Cinema, and Ethnographic Spectacle* (1996), Fatimah Rony asserts that the "Other" can never be an active critical agent and is not capable of being perceived as multidimensional or contradictory, "the Native Man in ethnographic cinema is not even perceived as being an actor: his performance is always 'real.' "[17] Even if desired, "postmodern" is simply not an available construct under these analyses, unless Native representatives relinquish their subjective identities as Native altogether. Here we fall into the "I'm an artist first, an Indian second" identity trap of having to prioritize one's subjectivity, a quandary that non-ethnic artists surely do not face.

Given these parameters, a venue such as the Venice Biennale might seem to offer little beyond reifying categories of Indianness. Native arts serve as a useful Other to established fine arts practices; as a pure local inserted into the cosmopolitanism of the global in the sense that the *International Herald Tribune* review positioned *Ceremonial*, or as a sorry convert to Western norms, a sanitized version of once colorful, exotic peoples. How can a transformative moment possibly be accomplished within these conceptual boundaries? The arguments that I have presented here suggest that an indigenous orientation can offer libratory potentials. Indigenous knowledge as a theoretical orientation suggests that a multivocal, processual, and participatory approach to global arts activism can avoid the liabilities of either legitimization through acculturation or rejection by the West. The problem is how to translate this theoretical orientation into practice—how to begin the process of education whereby indigenous participation in global initiatives is not about tokenism and does not rely upon tired interpretative tools.

Richard Ray Whitman asserted in *Umbilicus*, the NA3 exhibit for the 2001 Biennale: "We are asked to give, give, give. We respond by giving, giving, giving."[18] A responsibility to service is a central tenet of indigenous museum curation. Unfortunately, this "Red Man's Burden"[19] of helping others has extracted a cost by forcing Native art efforts to start with the ignorance of others, rather than Native self-wisdom. Is self-expression necessarily premised on dismantling the misconceptions of others who are unmotivated to relinquish their own comfort and control? Should Native artists and cultural workers commit to this burdensome task of cultural translations, given our often strained social, political, and economic capital? DuBois provocatively suggests that in response to racism, "A people thus handicapped ought not to be asked to race with the world, but rather allowed to give all its time and thought to its own social problems."[20] Why Venice? Why now?

Cultural Translations

The Native presence at the Venice Biennale has demonstrated how engagement with the global arena has positively served Native self-representation efforts. Rather than homogenizing cultural particularities under the rubric of globalization, the institution of the Venice Biennale offers both fluidity in global arts currents and continuation of the local-to-local relationships that are a hallmark of indigenous social norms. The Venetian people who have assisted Native arts endeavors over the course of four exhibitions and a number of years feel an affinity in our struggles for sovereignty. Venetian colleagues consider their city a sovereign body in relation to the nation-state of Italy. They are thus outraged when Native sovereignty efforts are denied. Our bond is defined by common political understandings about the environment, war, and the retention of cultural specificity. We enjoy food, friendship, our children growing, the passing of time, and observations about the art world. Venice has allowed a space that is non-totalitarizing. Within the existing constructs of this nationalistic venue, Native artists have taken themselves seriously. Exterior legitimization from the American press and major arts institutions once seemed valuable and important for the meaningful continuation of contemporary Native arts dialogues, but these parameters have ceased to carry as much weight. When once we wanted recognition, now the emerging cultural translations of "multiple art worlds" are sufficient.

One of the greatest compliments I received during the course of working together on multiple exhibitions in Venice came from Italian curator Mario di Martino during the 2003 project *Pellerossasogna*. Following the exhibit opening, a dozen or more people converged for a home-cooked dinner in the garden behind our shared apartment. The fish that I had purchased at the Rialto that morning was not overdone, and the pasta was light. After much eating, we sat back lazily in our chairs, laughing and visiting over cigarettes. As the sky grew dark, it began to rain softly, and we reluctantly made our way inside, carrying plates, glasses, half loaves of bread, and empty wine bottles. At the dining room table, Sherwin began to paint watercolors on scraps of paper. Some climbed to sit on the sills of the open windows, while others tossed cushions on the floor and relaxed. Laughter from a hallway phone conversation mixed with the sound of a radio played in the distance. Posters, photos, papers, luggage, shoes, wet clothes, backpacks, and dirty dishes surrounded us. Mario sighed contentedly and—smiling and waving his hand dramatically in the air—declared, "I feel like I'm in a Fellini film!"

These simple commonalities hold real promise for demonstrating how marginalized communities may adopt the Biennale for generative self-ends that enhance rather than diminish cultural concerns. In this fashion, we give, but we also receive.

Nancy Marie Mithlo (Chiricahua Apache) is Assistant Professor of Anthropology at Smith College, Northampton, Massachusetts, and Director of the Indigenous Arts Action Alliance (IA3).

NOTES

1. The arts collective NA3 sponsored three exhibits at the Venice Biennale—*Ceremonial* (1999), *Umbilicus* (2001), and, under its new title Indigenous Arts Action Alliance (IA3), *Pellerossasogna* (2003). For more on these efforts, see Nancy M. Mithlo, " 'We Have All Been Colonized': Subordination and Resistance on a Global Arts Stage," *Visual Anthropology* 17: 3–4 (2004): 229–45, and Mithlo, "Reappropriating Redskins: *Pellerossasogna* (Red Skin Dream): Shelley Niro at the 50th La Biennale di Venezia," *Visual Anthropology Review* 20: 2 (2005): 22–35.

2. Interview with author, 1999.

3. Luna made the comment in an interview with Blake Gopnik, "Indian Artists in Venice: Off the Traditional Path," *The Washington Post*, July 24, 2005.

4. See the Venice Biennale website: (http://www.labiennale.org/en/art/directors/storr/en/61002.html).

5. Salah M. Hassan and Olu Oguibe, *Authentic/Ex-Centric: Conceptualism in Contemporary African Art* (Ithaca: Forum for African Arts, 2001), 7.

6. Ibid., 6.

7. Ibid., 7.

8. Catherine A. Lutz and Jane Collins, *Reading National Geographic* (Chicago: University of Chicago Press, 1993).

9. Hassan and Oguibe, 22.

10. W. E. B. DuBois, "Strivings of the Negro People," *Atlantic Monthly* 80 (1897): 194.

11. Ibid., 197.

12. Speech by Davide Croff about the symposium *Where Art Worlds Meet.* See the Venice Biennale website (http://www.labiennale.org/en/art/directors/storr/en/61002.html).

13. Carlos Basualdo, comments at *Where Art Worlds Meet.*

14. Roderick Conway Morris, "Biennale Celebrates the Local," *International Herald Tribune,* June 12, 1999.

15. Claire Smith, Heather Burke, and Graeme K. Ward, "Globalisation and Indigenous Peoples: Threat or Empowerment?" in *Indigenous Cultures in an Interconnected World,* ed. Claire Smith and Graeme K. Ward (St. Leonards: Allen & Unwin, 2000), 1–24.

16. Philip J. Deloria, *Indians in Unexpected Places* (Lawrence: University Press of Kansas, 2004).

17. Fatimah Tobing Rony, *The Third Eye: Cinema, Race, and Ethnographic Spectacle* (Durham: Duke University Press, 1996), 178.

18. Richard Ray Whitman, *Umbilicus,* in *La Biennale di Venezia 49th Esposizione Internationale d'Arte: Platea dell'umanità - Plateau of Humankind - Plateau der Menschheit - Plateau de l'humanité,* eds. Harald Szeemann and Cecilia Liveriero Lavelli (Milano: Electa, 2001), 208–09.

19. Nancy Marie Mithlo, "Red Man's Burden: The Politics of Inclusion in the Museum Setting," *American Indian Quarterly* 28 (2004): 3–4.

20. DuBois, "Strivings of the Negro People," 197.

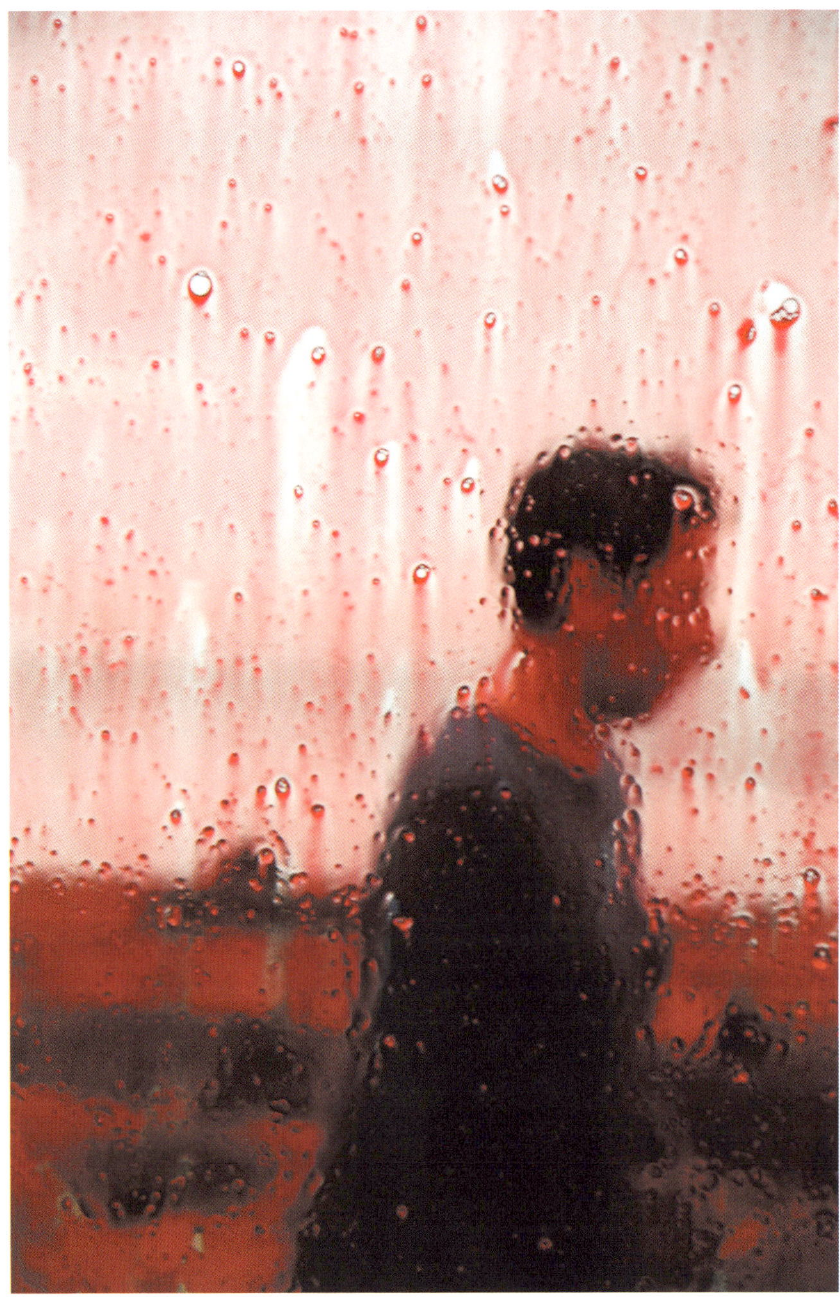

Rebecca Belmore (Anishinabe, b. 1960), *Fountain*, 2005. Production Still. Photo by José Ramón González. Image courtesy of the Morris and Helen Belkin Art Gallery.

LEE-ANN MARTIN

PERFORMANCE AND ARTISTIC MOBILITY

In the spirit of mobility and reciprocity that brought us to Venice for the symposium held by the National Museum of the American Indian (NMAI), I propose an alternate conceptual framework for the presentations in this session, for which I am acting as moderator. "Performance and Artistic Mobility" seems more suitable than "Performing Cultural Hybridity" in relation to contemporary Aboriginal art and curatorial practices, considering that the participants in this session traveled to this European destination from Aotearoa (New Zealand), Brazil, Canada, Turkey, and the United States, among other countries. Artists and curators, scholars, writers, and other cultural producers continuously travel throughout the globe. Traveling from one place to another, we constantly engage in rethinking our practices, not only within global contexts but also within the interstices between destinations. These transitional spaces are varied and always in flux, affording the opportunity to reflect upon our state of leaving and arriving.

Performance and Artistic Mobility is appropriate especially in relation to the performance practices of Rebecca Belmore (Anishinabe) and James Luna (Luiseño), whose representation in the 51st Venice Biennale inspired the National Museum of the American Indian's symposium. Belmore and Luna negotiate aesthetic spaces that combine performance and installation; autobiography and historiography; the local and the global. As contemporary artists, they too negotiate the transitional spaces associated with global travel. Physical and creative mobility define their performance practices and, yet, Belmore's *Fountain* and Luna's *Emendatio* were extraordinarily successful in addressing the cultural and historical particularities of Venice, of Italy, and of Europe. As the artists emplace themselves in Venice, they claim this space within their telling of Aboriginal history. Their symbolic acts further dramatize our intertwined history where, beginning in the seventeenth century, glass factories on Murano Island first manufactured glass beads for trade with Aboriginal peoples in the Americas. Indeed, historian Ronald Wright proclaims:

> The world we have today is the gift of the New World. We in the lucky countries of the West now regard our two-century bubble of freedom and affluence as normal and inevitable. Yet this new order is an anomaly. Our age was bankrolled by the seizing of half a planet, extended by taking over most of the remaining half, and has been sustained by spending down new forms of natural capital, especially fossil fuels. In the New World, the West hit the biggest bonanza of all time.[1]

Belmore's performance-based video installation, *Fountain*, seeks to shatter long-held atrocities embedded in our conflicted global history of colonial relations and contemporary interactions. On a significant European cultural and intellectual site, Belmore honors the memory of millions of people lost to hostile and violent intentions. In his performance for the mixed-media installation, *Emendatio*, Luna completes the cycle of Pablo Tac, a Luiseño youth who left California for Rome, Italy, more than one hundred and seventy years ago for studies to become a missionary and died there, never returning home. Over four days during the opening of the Biennale, Luna's performance provided a mediation of local and global human connections. In their performance practices, Belmore's and Luna's bodies broaden the scope of indigenous cultural histories beyond traditional and temporal definitions, and posit indigenous contemporary art practices squarely in a transglobal present-day. The body has emerged as a dominant subject of contemporary artistic practice in part to articulate cultural difference, as well as the history of colonialism that continues to resonate throughout the world. Today, the body is acknowledged as a complex, highly coded, shifting subject that lives within representation.[2]

Ironically, in the late 1980s in Canada and in the United States, Rebecca Belmore and James Luna first received national recognition for dramatic performances that immobilized their bodies as "artifacts." As specimens in museumified environments, their bodies reify what Paul Chaat Smith describes as the conflation of Indians with the things we made, and with the fictions that others made up: "If there is any people on earth whose lives are more tangled up with museums than we are, God help them."[3]

In 1988, Belmore created *Artifact #671B* in support of the Lubicon Cree First Nation of northern Alberta. The Lubicon sought an international boycott of *The Spirit Sings: Artistic Traditions of Canada's First Peoples*, an exhibition at the Glenbow Museum in celebration of the 1988 Olympics in Calgary, Alberta. The highly publicized boycott brought international attention to the Lubicon Cree's outstanding claim to land that the major sponsor of the exhibition, Shell Oil, was happily exploiting for oil and profits. On January 12, 1988, in -18°C weather, Belmore sat immobile as *Artifact #671B* for two hours on the frozen ground in a life-sized museum case outside the Thunder Bay Art Gallery in northern Ontario. Her performance expressed the collective anger of many Aboriginal people throughout Canada who angrily condemned the exhibition's organizers and sponsor for perpetuating the romanticization of Aboriginal cultural history while ignoring the complex contemporary realities of Aboriginal communities.

In 1987, James Luna performed his groundbreaking work, *The Artifact Piece*, at the San Diego Museum of Man in California. For this first masterpiece, Luna lay motionless, with closed eyes, for hours in an open museum case—the dead Indian—complete with identification labels to contextualize the particular incidents whereby the Indian received his various scars and bruises. The Indian's possessions (material culture) were displayed in adjacent cases to further contextualize the Indian's life. Luna's "material culture objects" included books by such authors as Kerouac and Ginsberg, and music cassettes by the Sex Pistols and Hank Williams. After viewing dioramas of so many neutralized and aestheticized museological misrepresentations of "things Indian," the visitor encountered Luna's objectified body—shocking in its living immediacy and confrontation with the perpetuation of museological myths about the American Indian.

At the symposium, Jean Fisher noted that people, not places, are the sites of art. Belmore's and Luna's bodies are powerful registers of history and lived experiences, of endurance and resistance, of decimation and imagination. As such, their bodies are complex metaphors for, and inseparable from, contemporary realities and memories of historical conflicts. Their practices are potent challenges to Western mythic traditions of indigenous authenticity and history.

In the end, I am perplexed by the question of what it means for indigenous artists from the Americas to (re)present themselves at the Venice Biennale. The answer is as simple as the time, resources, and choices individuals need to travel from their homes. It is also as complex as being an indigenous person in this neo-colonial world.

Lee-Ann Martin (Mohawk) is Curator of Contemporary Canadian Aboriginal Art at the Canadian Museum of Civilization, Gatineau, Quebec.

NOTES

1. Ronald Wright, *A Short History of Progress* (Toronto: House of Anansi Press, 2004), 115–17.

2. Bruce Grenville, *Body: New Art from the UK* (London and Vancouver: The British Council and Vancouver Art Gallery, 2005).

3. Paul Chaat Smith, "Luna Remembers," in *James Luna: Emendatio* (Washington, D.C.: National Museum of the American Indian, Smithsonian Institution, 2005), 33.

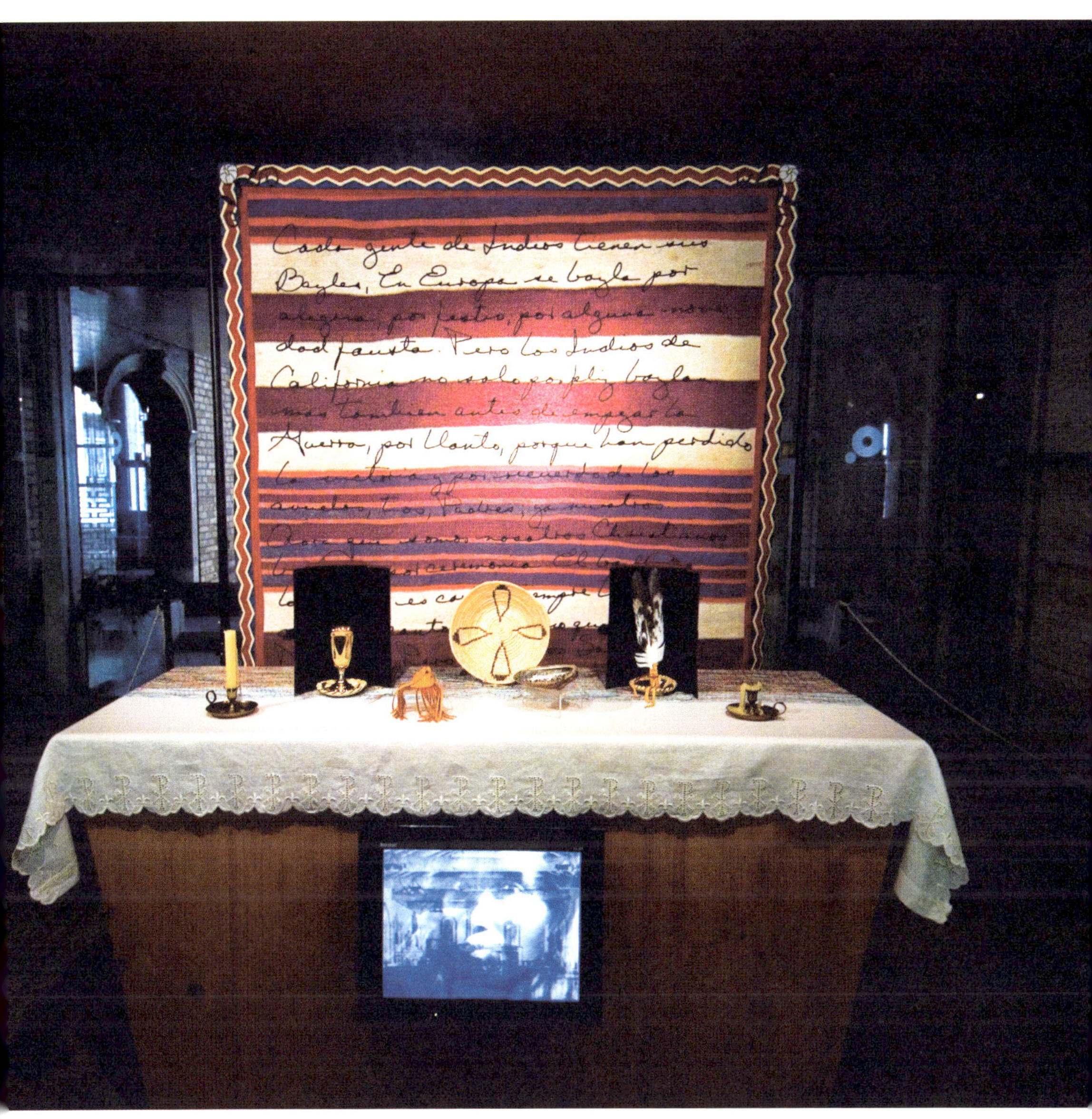

"Chapel for Pablo Tac," one of two installations for *Emendatio* by James Luna (Luiseño, b. 1950), at the 2005 Venice Biennale. Photo by Katherine Fogden. © NMAI.

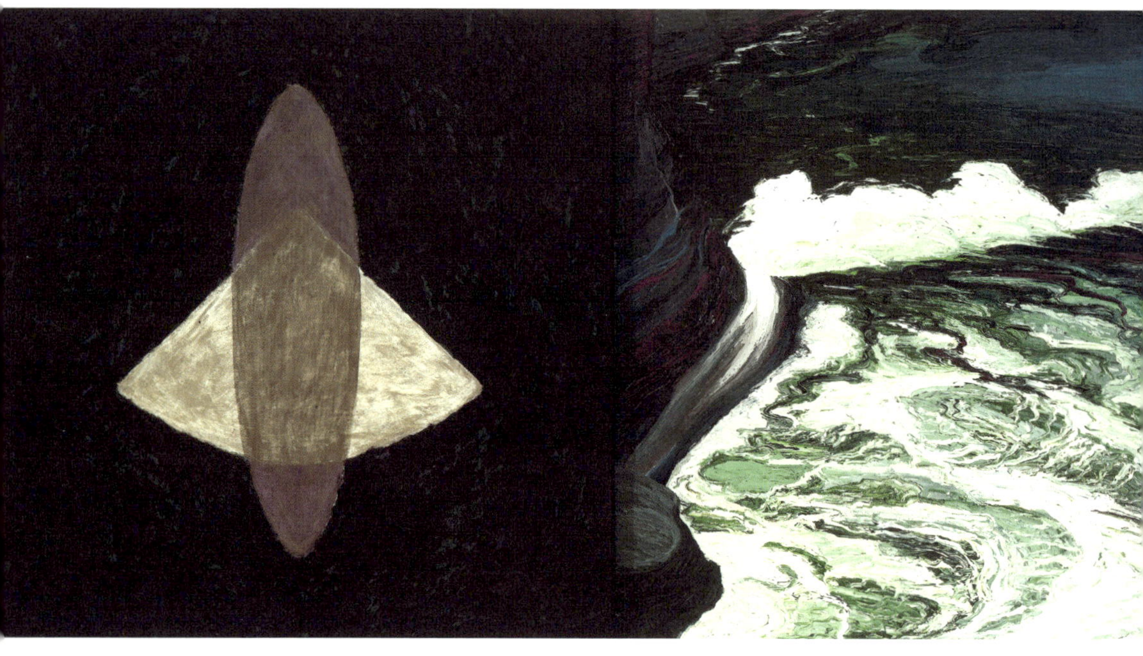

Kay WalkingStick (Cherokee, b. 1935), *Letting Go / From Chaos to Calm*, 1990. Acrylic, wax, oil on canvas, 121.9 x 243.8 cm. Collection of the Rockwell Museum of Western Art, Richard Florsheim Art Fund and Clara S. Peck Fund purchase. Photo by Cascadilla Photo. © Kay WalkingStick.

SYLVIE FORTIN

A Generative Map

Some of what I have to say here has already been said over the last four days. How could it be otherwise? But please follow me as I attempt to reframe or align things slightly differently to highlight facets that have not yet been explored here and move the discussion forward. The symposium organizers have asked us to "aim to open new possibilities, share new ideas, produce unexpected insights, and map new directions for the future"; I have taken this prospective orientation very seriously.

Prospections, however, always have to be anchored in a particular time and place. We must therefore start with a precise and critical analysis of where I think we are now. In the spirit of provoking thought, dialogue, and learning in public, here are some reflections that hopefully will amount to a generative map to be contested and twisted.

A few preliminary remarks are in order. In many of the discussions over the past few days, I was struck by the fact that two things seem to be constantly confused: artistic and curatorial work or practice is conflated with institutional and market recognition. I think we really need to unbind these two things. They are not always equivalent, and they don't always coincide. I know it is simple, but it is crucial. Such conflation is deadly for the development of programs in any institution that seeks to contribute to something other than the hegemony of global capital. Although practice and recognition do sometimes converge, they remain radically different and it is essential for any institution that aspires to be anything more than a show-case to remember this.

I would like to make another remark, this time about biennials. The word entails some cycle of recurrence, a desire to live on every two years. For the discussion here, I will use the term "biennial" simply to mean large-scale international exhibition. The many different types of these projects are often grouped under some vague notion of internationalism, and what does that really mean? If you have two nations, that constitutes international. So we need to be more precise.

The term is now used for a wide array of projects that aspire to grasp various regionalisms; here we can talk about a whole range of biennials within the United States. We can also talk about European biennials, such as Manifesta, or Nordic European biennials such as Momentum, various Asia-Pacific events, Caribbean biennials, and so on. Sometimes the alignment is political, sometimes it is economic, and at times it is both. Other examples assume, or try to assume, a global stance; here, I think in particular of Documenta.

Now I would like to address the questions posed by the symposium organizers, beginning with, "Is the work done by non-Western contemporary artists, for example, still being reduced to ethnic or racial lines?" And I am collapsing this question with another, "Is there a trend toward inclusion of non-Western artists in major, mainstream contemporary art exhibitions?" I would say that the work done by non-Western artists is not reduced to ethnic or racial lines, but it is processed through that prism, and this produces a difference. These factors, like other biographical factors such as gender, age, and class, do produce and set up sets of expectations—both stated and unstated—that deeply inflect the conditions of visibility, inclusion, and potency of the work and its location in a curator's conceptual map, as well as in the spatial text that is the exhibition. The way that Rosa Martinez's exhibition at the Arsenale for this year's Venice Biennale foregrounded the feminist agenda by using a Guerilla Girls poster right up front provides a good example. That can be a strategy—it can also be lethal, especially when it is a strategy that you repeat with every show. Another important point to make is that in many shows that claim to be global, works from the so-called margin are relegated to secondary, peripheral rooms that you can easily miss. A spatial translation of conceptual modes is at work that sometimes people are aware of and sometimes not.

A trend to inclusion for the sake of representativity is current now. This inclusion does not encompass understanding, learning, mediating, or presenting the work in such a way that it can truly release its critical potential. Formal parameters still often guide the inclusion of work from cultures and places with which a curator is less familiar. An inclusion, especially in large-scale biennials, frequently coincides with what I call the curatorial yellow pages, which is the established list of foreign artists on whom one calls to guarantee the global character and legitimacy of one's exhibition. Often you only need to have one such artist. Now, if you need two, hopefully you will pick a woman second or a representative of different religion or ethnic group—and if you can have both in one, then so much the better.

Panelists were also asked, "Is the Western or mainstream art institution still a site of struggle for non-Western artists?" Yes and no. The mainstream art institution has to be understood as a very complex and constantly adapting system. It differentiates itself and adapts very rapidly. Some encounters are slick and some are striated. We like to think of museums as mausoleums or dinosaurs—and in a way they are. Geeta Kapur spoke eloquently of the lack of infrastructure for the arts in countries such as India and of the role that biennials could come to play in such context. I welcome and agree with that statement. On the other hand, we must not lose sight of another very important factor, which is the historical moment of emergence of large-scale biennials. We spoke extensively, earlier on, about the emergence of the Havana Biennial in 1984. One thing that was not stated, however, was that this coincided precisely with the resurgence of painting in mainstream Western institutions on the one hand and building campaigns by museums on the other. I think that, yes, there was a desire for South-to-South dialogue, but we need to complexify that and understand that at the same time in the so-called mainstream art world and in terms of the development of institutions, something else was also going on that involved the shaping of global capital. We need to modulate all of these things somewhat differently.

An interesting hypothesis about the emergence of biennials might be found in the fact that the time of their emergence is precisely the moment when experimentations from the '60s and '70s vanished from mainstream institutions. They go underground through this channel of biennials to reappear in the 1990s. Now, what about the proliferation of biennials in the '90s? Again, that coincides with the fact that so many Western museums were closed for renovation at the same time. That is something that very few people bring into the equation. It is not just that all of a sudden there were plentiful resources; it is also that a lot of places were closed. One example is *Rendezvous: Masterpieces from the Centre Georges Pompidou and the Guggenheim Museums* (October 14, 1998–January 24, 1999), an important exhibition that was in New York when the Pompidou Center was closed in Paris. Basically, the Pompidou Center shipped their collection elsewhere, made something like twelve million dollars, and didn't have to pay for storage or insurance. This is all related and needs to be brought into the equation.

To wrap up that hypothesis very briefly: the biennial developed as an outsourced, globally distributed and inexpensive interim museum. Biennials were mobile sites of legitimization that through their distribution would not challenge the centrality of museums. We may not be comfortable yet with such close comparison, this sort of raw economics, but I believe that we need to do so.

Perhaps we can agree on a couple of more obvious points. Biennials have relieved the pressure on museums. Now museums don't have to perform certain functions because there is this other outlet that takes care of these tasks. Thus, museums in the United Kingdom can get away with the fashion of doing one Africa show every ten years. Or you do one Brazil show at the Guggenheim, and you charge the Brazilian government a lot of money for it. That is where we are at right now in terms of this kind of balance and distribution of power and resource.

The network of biennials at present might be best understood as a branch of the vertically integrated global art institution whose practices are not too different, for example, from those of multinational pharmaceutical or biotech companies. More concisely, we are witnessing two practices: one is dumping, and the second is what I call the monoculture of the multicultural. This in turn creates many challenges; for instance, you end up having "biennial artists," which is this list of artists who are essentially interchangeable. Biennials can now be thought of as kind of subsidiaries that have been put in place the world over to provide outlets and channels for asporic artists and artists working in so-called peripheries to each type of biennial and its own peripheries. The regional European biennials will have Eastern Europe as their periphery, while the Whitney Biennial will have the regions of America as its peripheries, and so forth.

We were also asked, "Why is it that the non-Western contemporary artist can belong neither to the West nor to modernity?" The choice of the verb "belonging" is puzzling to me; I don't really know what it means in this question. To me, a better choice of word would have been "shaping." Why can't we see it as, "Why can't the contemporary non-Western artist be seen as both shaping the West and shaping modernity?" Just something to think about.

I also thought, What was I to make of this invitation by the National Museum of the American Indian to come here to Venice? I viewed the invitation as a way to come together, work through strategies, and propose strategies for the future. I will start out by stating a few values and then a few hypotheses. Amid the shifting and reconfiguring terrain of contemporary art—cutting through the hype, the promises, the allure, the inflation—what matters to me is to ensure the emergence and development of sustainable practices, be they artistic, curatorial, academic, or other. To curate not only artworks but also to generate practices—certainly not to inflate careers. To me, the only true profitable investment is fostering research; most important, the production and dissemination of ideas, works, exhibitions, texts, and audiences. It is not the spectacle of the event or the buzz of the career, but the production of space—and here I think we come back to the line in the sand that Paul so eloquently described. It is not about fitting into a space, but about producing a space.

So what is to be done? Speaking here to and about the National Museum of the American Indian (NMAI), I do think that these are exciting times because the institution is still inventing itself. A window of opportunity is still open, but, given the nature of institutions, it will more than likely shut down very soon. You must seize the opportunity to put in place sustainable structures to allow for an ongoing investigation of what contemporary Native art can be and how it can be manifested. And I do think that this has to happen structurally. If it doesn't happen structurally, it cannot be sustained. I think it is important to create and allocate resources to some kind of autonomous shape-shifting structure within the institution, which is to be understood as a site of experimentation, a site from which internal pressures on the institution might be exerted. But it must be a platform that can respond to changes in external conditions as well. The convergence of this symposium in Venice under the aegis of the NMAI and the recent programs of the museum mean that it is a priority of the institution to create much-needed visibility for Native and Aboriginal artists. I couldn't agree more.

Jolene Rickard eloquently said this morning that what matters is to reimagine indigenous space on a global scale, and that is precisely what we are talking about. My recommendation is certainly not to latch onto a vehicle that has already run out of gas, but to develop new, precise, nimble, and multiple vehicles. I would put back to the institution the question: Is any site so dominant today as to warrant the concentrative investment of intellectual, artistic, institutional, and financial resources? Once, yes; always, no. Venice is not enough—mobile and multiple platforms are needed to break the isolation to which many Native practices are confined and build manifold connections within and outside Aboriginal communities in the United States and the world.

I think that it is absolutely essential to develop a network of research and production residencies that can be mobile sites for Native artists in collaboration with local institutions around the world. Another priority is to develop a number of curatorial research residencies for Native and non-Native curators to enable them to familiarize themselves with the work of Native artists throughout the United States and the Americas. Again, this could be tied back to the related institutions through lecture programs and so on. The creation of a serious journal of contemporary Native art is also crucial so that there is, beyond the exhibition catalogue, an ongoing site of reflection that is not tied to your programs. This discourse and dialogue production exceeds what we can program within walls, even if they are mobile walls. Here one model is certainly *Nka: Journal of Contemporary African Art*; another model is *Les Cahiers du Musée national d'art moderne* at the Pompidou Center in Paris. Again, it is about transcending the exhibition programming. And, finally—the model here is the Arab Image Foundation, which has managed to do tremendous work in a very short period of time—contemporary Native art research centers that include accessible databases should be developed in collaboration with select universities around the world.

My last point, a most important one, is that every institution concerned with contemporary artists should start fostering a new patronage base. And I am talking way beyond collection; I am talking about different ways of fostering support from a range of constituents who are the audience with which we want to be in touch. Many people do not know about the different ways in which they can support art; they think that the only way they can accomplish this is by buying things. We have to do a much better job at inviting them into the conversation and building connections because that is what it is really about. I talk to many collectors who say, apologetically, that they don't collect for investment; they collect for the connection that they feel. If a connection that matters in a social way is important to our supporters, they can contribute to programs in various ways—and we need to illuminate the ways. Again, as Jolene said this morning, How do we make small work for us? These five options are small ways that I think could work for us.

Sylvie Fortin is the editor-in-chief of Art Papers *magazine in Atlanta, Georgia.*

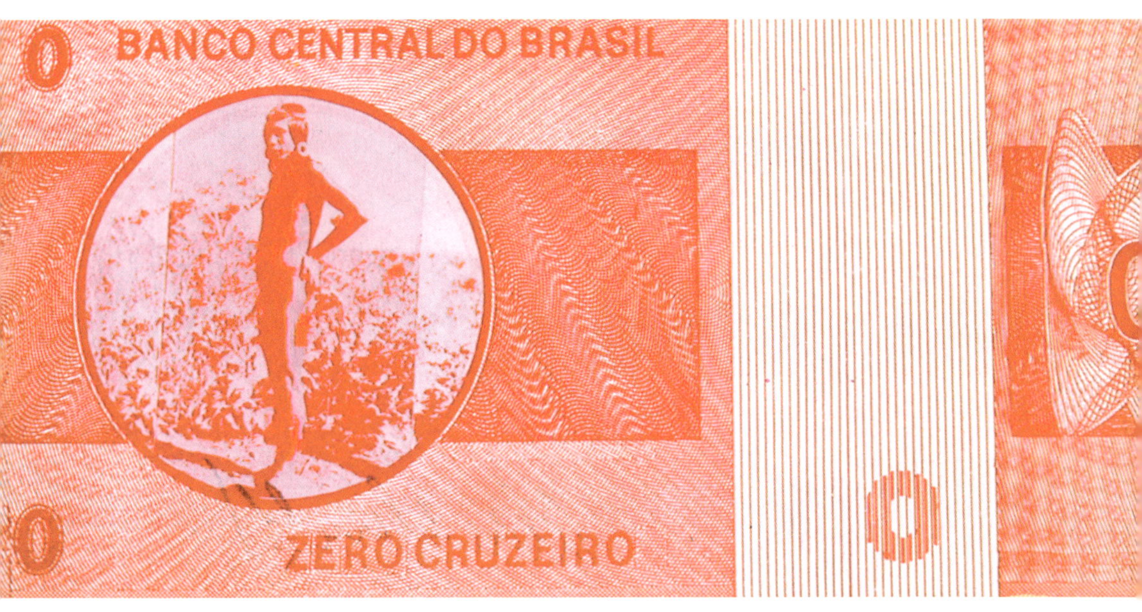

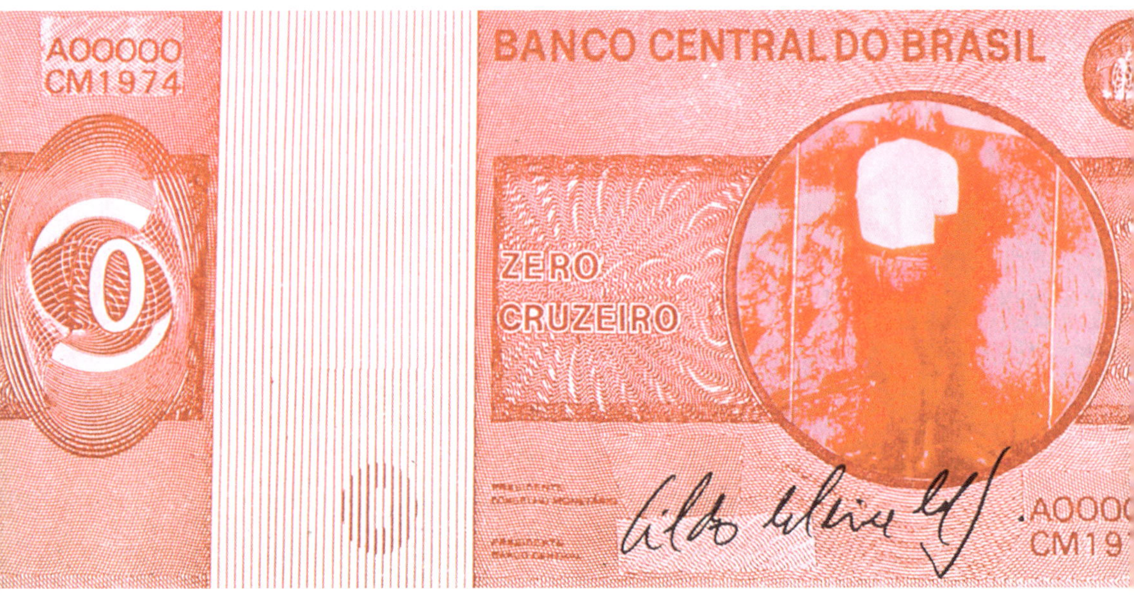

Cildo Meireles (Brazilian, b. 1948), *Zero Cruzeiro*, from the series *Inserções em Circuitos Ideologicos / Insertions into Ideological Circuits*, 1974–78. Unlimited edition double-sided print, 7 x 15 cm. Donated by Gabriela Salgado, UECLAA # 444. © University of Essex Collection of Latin American Art.

PAULO HERKENHOFF

THE THIRD BANK OF THE RIVER:
ART AND THE INDIGENOUS PEOPLE OF BRAZIL

In "The Third Bank of the River," a short story by Brazilian writer João Guimarães Rosa (1908–1967), the narrator's father, orderly and positive, a quiet man who honored his duties, has a one-person boat, sturdy enough to last for some twenty or thirty years, built for himself.[1] Bidding goodbye to his family, he sets off for the river, taking neither food nor clothing. The son asks his father to take him along, but the father only blesses him.

The father never returned; yet he went nowhere. He just rowed and floated out there on the river. He would be seen sometimes. The son feared that his father would get lost in the rapids, but then would see him in his boat, calmly under the trees. The neighbors were disgusted by his behavior. Was this a vow, a promise? Was it destiny? Was it leprosy? Was he mad? The narrator's sister and mother depart from the village, leaving only the son to accompany his father on his journey to nowhere. One day the son, growing white-haired himself, calls to his father and, as the boat approaches the bank, asks to replace him. Yet the son then flees, asking himself, "Why was I guilty?"

As my description reveals, "The Third Bank of the River" expresses a sense of strangeness—the Freudian *unheimlich*—and a fear of the unconscious. Is the precarious "nowhere" of the story that of the void of modernity that Brazilian artist Hélio Oiticica (1937–1980) invoked when he wrote "from adversity we live"? Does it refer to the "precariousness of being" that Lygia Clark (1920–1988), another artist from Brazil, puts into her experience of art? We do know that the river is a symbol of time—the passage of time—as either memory or history. In this symposium, it seems to me, we are asking who is on the third bank of the river.

Origins

Brazilian conceptual artist Cildo Meireles created a work called *Zero Cruzeiro* (1974–78), based on the Brazilian cruzeiro, which had been devalued due to hyperinflation. In the central portion of the note—the place where figures from heroic, official history are usually depicted—Meireles puts images of a mentally-ill person and of a Kraô (a Brazilian Native). The artist represents them as members of two social groups ascribed no productive value by capitalism and Brazilian society. Could the zero value in Meireles's work be the third bank of the river? The writer and the artist, respectively, investigate the meaning of the third bank and the zero as the social place for madness. For João Guimarães Rosa, the father means the "origin." Meireles focuses the very notion of "origin" on the Natives—there lies the origin of Brazil. The *Zero Cruzeiro* leads us to other issues.

The Meireles family has long been engaged in the protection of Indian territories. Cildo Meireles rejects the eighteenth-century idea of the "beau sauvage." "Before Portugal discovered Brazil, Brazil had discovered felicity," wrote Brazilian poet and polemicist Oswald de Andrade in the *Manifesto Antropófago* (Cannibal Manifesto) in 1928. "Antropofagia" is a modernist concept that posits Brazilian culture as being formed through the absorption of all contributions—but mainly from Natives, African slaves, and European settlers. The concept is derived from the idea of cannibalism as a ceremonial practice of the Natives of Brazil for the absorption of the qualities of the enemy. Yet the contributions of indigenous people and Afro-descendants are confined by Brazilian aristocratic modernism within the old frame of appropriation—a platform of "national art" that uses the elite's symbolic construction of subaltern and dominated social groups.

In this regard, Cildo Meireles and Swiss-born photographer Claudia Andujar represent a major ethical change in Brazilian art since the 1970s. Andujar has lived among the Yanomami of the Amazon Basin for many years and has played a leading role—both in Brazil and in the international arena—in efforts to secure the definition and defense of the Yanomami territories. She has denounced genocidal movements. Her photography has been at the service of the Yanomami for more than three decades, and she shares with them the economic results of her projects about them. Andujar has made works that show the affability of the Yanomami and the spiritual beauty of their cosmogonic vision and point out the cultural entropy and death tolls resulting from the forced integration of Yanomamis with Brazilian national society.

Cildo Meireles has created a large number of works dealing with the historical condition of Native people under Portuguese colonization and Brazilian national society. *Cruzeiro do Sul* (1969–70), for example, is a tiny cube made of two kinds of wood, soft pine and hard oak—materials used by Native people to make fire. Meireles says that when a lighter is introduced into some Native communities, their mythology is torn apart. Meireles's *Cruzeiro do Sul* precedes *The Anti-Oedipus* (1972) by the French philosopher Gilles Deleuze and psychoanalyst Félix Guattari, a book that discusses the relationship between capitalism and schizophrenia.

Missão/Missões (How to Build Cathedrals) of 1987 refers to the Jesuit missions established among the Guarani Indians in Paraguay, Argentina, and Brazil beginning in 1609. Symbolizing the relationship between wealth, agricultural exploitation, and religion, Meireles's "cathedral" has a floor made of 600,000 coins and a ceiling of 2,000 cattle bones, connected by a column of 800 communion wafers. The Catholic missions could be seen as ideological pathways to the colonial conquest.

In the first half of the seventeenth century, the Dutch established the West India Company in Pernambuco, in the northeastern part of Brazil. They brought in the most multifaceted group of artists and scientists in the Americas at that moment, including artists such as Frans Janszoon Post (Dutch, 1612–1680), who painted landscapes depicting nature and colonial architecture, and Albert Eckhout (Dutch, ca. 1610–1665). Eckhout was the first painter of the flora of Brazil and can also be acknowledged for the first pictorial renderings of Brazilian ethnic diversity. He painted images of male-female couples from various groups in the population: the Tupi Indians, the Tapuya Indians, Africans, and mulattos and mestizos. The symbolic aspects of those paintings are remarkable.

The indigenous people portrayed in *Tapuyas* (1641) were considered very fierce, as symbolized by the beast (a sharp-toothed dog) placed by the central figure of a woman. The vegetation, seen through European eyes, is menacing. The woman is placed in a position of sexual enticement. In the background, visible through her legs, we see Native warriors going to battle. She has picked fruits and holds some human body parts, including a foot and a hand. Clearly, she represents a cannibal. Eckhout's *Tupi* (1643) depicts an affectionate woman with her child. In the background, we see that her community has joined the colonial process in agriculture. She is seen as productive because she stands beside a banana tree. Another banana tree has been cut by a blade, signifying the presence of European "civilization." She carries some complex artifacts, a sign of material culture. She is dressed in a skirt. For all these reasons, she would not be seen as a cannibal. According to the anthropologist Ronald Raminelli, however, Eckhout was wrong. In spite of their aggression, the Tapuyas were not cannibals, and despite their domesticity, the Tupinambás, from the group of the Tupis, were cannibals on a symbolic, ritualistic level.

The representation of Native culture has evolved through the centuries in Brazilian culture. A Nativist literature emerged. In the mid nineteenth century, painting also started to represent the Native. The "beau sauvage," however, was nude. Nudity was acceptable under the model of the Chateaubriand Indian or in Christianizing situations, as in *The First Mass of Brazil* (1861), painted by Victor Meirelles de Lima, which is considered the primal scene of the country, or in *The Last Tamoio* (1883) by Rodolfo Amoedo. These works of art were crucial in the symbolic formation of Brazil as a national society.

Representations of Africans and Natives

The representation of the Native could not be separated from the representation of the African in Brazil. In Eckhout's painting of an African woman (1641), her attributes indicate her economic functions as a slave. She works to provide food, as shown by the fruit-filled basket she holds, and she breeds new slaves, symbolized by the child who stands beside her. The child holds two objects: a parrot—a voice without a soul, as slaves and Indians were viewed at the time—and a corncob, which used to be the only food eaten during the day in the mining areas of Minas Gerais in the eighteenth century, according to some historical data. The main attribute is the "third bank" of the ocean. It is seen at her back in the painting, which means that her origin is forever left behind. As Argentinean philosopher Saul Karsz has observed, the time process for a slave is an absolute severance from the past.

Brazil did not abolish slavery until 1888. José Ferraz de Almeida Júnior (1850–1899), the official painter for the new coffee aristocracy in São Paulo, was considered one of the most important genre painters of Brazil. During the time he was painting, the immigrant was being substituted for the slave. It was a moment in which the African was pictured as unreliable and lazy, a negative image projected in order to favor bringing in immigrants as paid labor. In Almeida Junior's somehow racist paintings, there are no blacks—only whites and or the *caipiras*, hybrid descendants of the Native. In his oeuvre, Natives were tolerated only as faraway, dissolved, and vague vestiges—not as a true presence. More interesting, Modesto Brocos (1800–1900), a Spanish painter who moved to Brazil, extensively represented the life of the blacks in Brazil, both as individuals and as a social group. In *The Redemption of Cam* (1895), a critical Brocos depicted the acceptance of the theory of whitening by a former woman slave who praises the fact that, through the marriage of her mestizo daughter, her grandson is even whiter. Brocos created a document of these wishes among Afro-descendants in order for them to escape social prejudice and exclusion in Brazil. Until Brocos, the only portrait of a black individual with a name in the nineteenth century is *The Brave Sailor Simão, Coalman of the Steamship Pernambucana,* painted by Jose Correia de Lima not long before he died in 1857. Simão had to be a hero to deserve a half-length portrait; he saved many lives when his ship was wrecked along the coast of Brazil. The exclusion of the indigenous population and of the former slaves was deeply intermingled in Brazil.

In the past, some art critics have argued that there was no art production among Brazilian Natives. This problematic position is partially explained by the negative ideological pressure on the identity of Natives and their descendants living in urban centers; many chose to deny their origin in order to survive the scourges of ethnocentrism. There have, in fact, been indigenous artists such as the painter Chico da Silva (1910-1985).

Evolving Creativity

Today, Native groups and individuals throughout Brazil have gained access to video technology, which they are using as a means of self-expression. This has resulted in a tremendous output of documentary and fictional films. The documentary *Shomõtsi* (2001), directed by Valdete Pinhanta Ashenika, chronicles events in the life of an Ashaninka Indian living in the state of Acre, on the border of Brazil and Peru. The 2003 film *Kinja Iakaha, A Day in the Village* was directed by Araduwá Waimiri, Iawusu Waimiri, Kabaha Waimiri, Sanapyty Atroari, Sawá Waimiri, and Wamé Atroari. The six videomakers of different Waimiri and Atroari villages in the Amazon document the day-to-day life of their relatives in the Cacau village, guided by their deep respect for the environment.

Filmmakers, painters, and other artists, taking pride in their indigenous origin and heritage, are making visible the "third bank" of Brazilian culture. It is a major change in the arts that we hope will bring great results. One such artist is Pituku Waiapi, a Waiapi from the Amapá. Pituku has suffered from polio and, according to tribal rules, he should have been sacrificed. Instead, he was taken away by Fundação Nacional do Indio (FUNAI), an agency for the protection of the Natives, to Belém. Unable to walk, he uses a wheelchair. He had to learn to paint with a brush held in his mouth. He dedicates his painting to representing fundamental aspects of his cultural group, such as the shaman, the symbolism of body painting, and his village (the *aldeia*). Pituku is now a professional artist who derives his earnings from his painting. Art has rescued him, and he now can return and stay with his family. Pituku says that he was longing for his aldeia when he was painting. He addresses his paintings-in-progress in the Waiapi language to ask them what is necessary. Pituku swears that his paintings answer him only in Waiapi.

Art critic and independent curator Paulo Herkenhoff was formerly Director of the Museu Nacional de Belas Artes, Rio de Janeiro, Brazil.

NOTES

1. João Guimarães Rosa, "The Third Bank of the River," trans. William L. Grossman, in Roberto González Echevarría, ed., *The Oxford Book of Latin American Short Stories* (New York: Oxford University Press, 1997), 256–60.

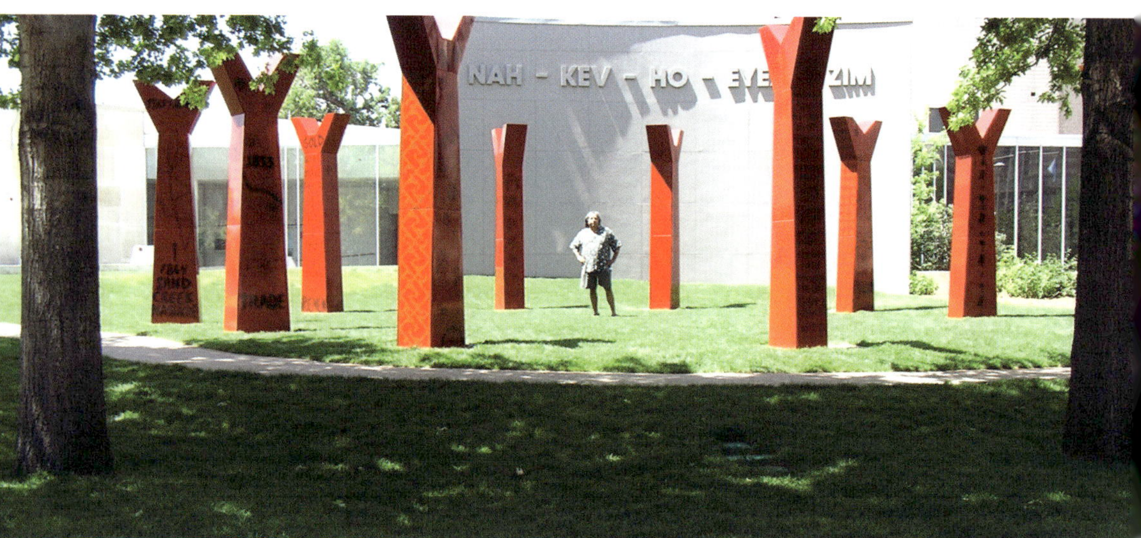

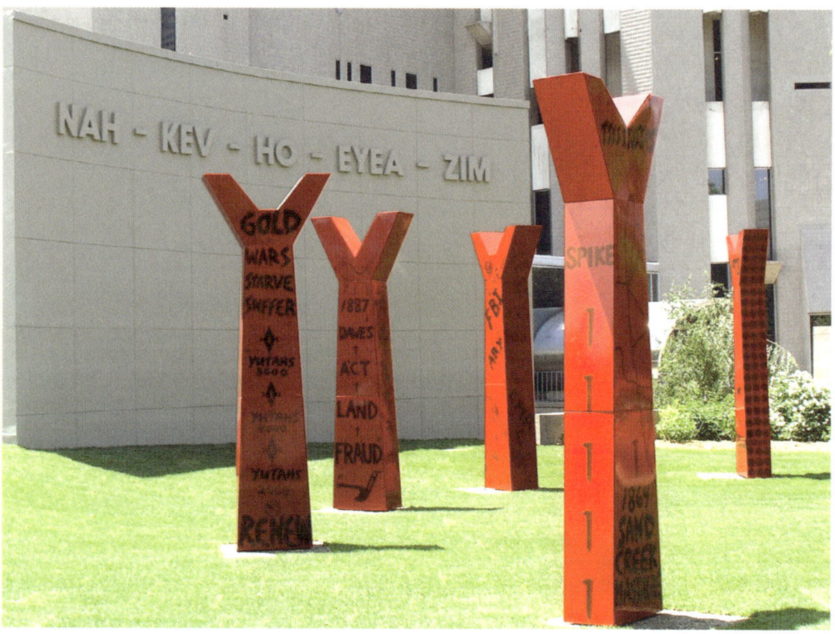

HOCK E AYE VI Edgar Heap of Birds (Cheyenne/Arapaho, b. 1954), *Wheel*, 2005. Porcelain on steel, 365.8 x 61 cm (each tree). Collection of the Denver Art Museum. Funds from Charles J. Norton by exchange, and funds from the Bonfils-Stanton Foundation, the AT&T Foundation, the National Endowment for the Arts, and the Douglas Society. 1997.145.

Top: Artist HOCK E AYE VI Edgar Heap of Birds pictured with *Wheel*, June 2005. Photo © Shanna Ketchum. Bottom: Detail view of *Wheel*, June 2005. Photo © HOCK E AYE VI Edgar Heap of Birds.

ROBERT HOULE

Creating Space Within a National Identity

Being born in a country whose national identity excludes your history and culture complicates the development of your personal identity. Being an artist of the first peoples of the Western Hemisphere places your art outside the cultural norm of Western civilization—a placement reinforced through Christopher Columbus's original misrecognition of the indigenous people he encountered as being from India. The European invention of the "New World," the template on which the idea of America is constructed, comes from the legacy of fifteenth century Vatican papal bulls.[1]

It is a case of being inside yet outside that makes the current discourse of postcolonialism, the assertion that all of the people on this earth have a right to the same material and cultural well-being, seem like hollow rhetoric. For the indigenous nations of America, colonialism is not "post" but "neo"; none of them have achieved full sovereignty. A national identity in which we are considered foreign is superimposed on our identities—for we are a multitude of peoples, nations, tribes, cultures, and histories.

The feeling of rejection and frustration experienced in being part of a nation yet not really enjoying its nourishing embrace from within is debilitating, leaving a tension between memory and desire. Any inference to inclusion is an illusion. Realistically, at the end of the day, the very idea of a Puritan America with a pagan past is a heretical notion that is far from ever becoming a cultural norm.

An artist identified with the first Americans of the United States views the mythology of Manifest Destiny and Columbus Day differently from other Americans. The indigenous idea of seeing Turtle Island as America is perhaps the bicultural hybridity that is Native America, a legitimate cultural construct of creation, the raison d'etre that places us in the scheme of things.

Cultural hybridity and multiculturalism are premises derived from a dominant viewpoint that indigenous art needs to be viewed, contextualized, and marketed ethnocentrically, outside of the national culture. Although this methodology is largely disputed, it is nevertheless intricately woven into how museums classify Native American art. The period of extraordinary European expansion in the eighteenth and nineteenth centuries led to a dominant world position that has now been transferred to North America, specifically the United States, leaving Native American art confined inside an imperial power.

It is crucial to add that not only contemporary feminism but also discussions of race relations and multiculturalism are undergirded by the premise that the withholding of recognition is a form of oppression. The voiceless invisibility of Native America in the country's national identity persists despite the enormous image-making industry of Disney and Hollywood. Cultural analysis has largely been the domain of Western anthropologists, art historians, cultural theorists, curators, critics, and connoisseurs; however, the recent desire to have a dialogue and recognize marginalized artists, curators, and scholars has given indigenous people the opportunity to participate, bringing their unique perspectives into the conversation.

Through Barnett Newman's sensitive cross-cultural observations and Jackson Pollock's perceptive analogy of ritual art,[2] the bicultural aspect found in some of their works demands to be compared to such Native American artists as Kay WalkingStick (Cherokee), James Lavadour (Walla Walla), Hulleah Tsinhnahjinnie (Diné/Seminole/Muscogee), and Edgar Heap of Birds (Cheyenne/Arapaho). Both WalkingStick and Lavadour have created landscapes profoundly influenced by the doctrines of psychic improvisation and automatism in the desire to draw upon and release the universal creativity of the unconscious mind, the surrealist roots of abstract expressionism. The sensuous qualities of the painting materials and the techniques of their manipulation in WalkingStick's *Letting Go, from Chaos to Calm* (1990) are a modest abstraction of inner strength that can be found when one feels abandoned after a loss of a life partner.[3] In Lavadour's *Deep Moon* (2004), the concept of "holistic" composition as a unified configuration of intimately related parts is a monumental abstraction with a process-driven image speaking more than ever of the subjective logic of artistic vision.[4]

A Process of Change

Current discourse provides a language and a politics in which Native American artists can question any imposed or superimposed image or representation. Making a radical ideological challenge to the authority and authenticity of a national identity requires a process of change. Splintered by modernity, anthropological theories that have legitimized the economic and cultural supremacy of the West must be openly questioned; the idea that all creativity of value must be of European provenance is a superiority complex, perhaps one of the most demeaning and dysfunctional agents of self-image. Exclusion is emigration from ancestral homelands, a diaspora where cultural assimilation and extinction are the emotional and violent realities of inequality.

Have you ever felt that the moment you speak, someone else has spoken for you? Or that when you hear others speaking, you are only going to be the object of their speech? Imagine living in a world of others, a world that exists for others, a world made real only because you have been spoken to. The construction of a healthy and positive self-image is made exceedingly difficult by the confounding fallacies of stereotyping and discrimination. Canadian philosopher Charles Taylor writes: "The thesis is that our identity is partly shaped by recognition or its absence, often by the misrecognition of others, and so a person or group of people can suffer real damage, real distortion, if the people or society around them mirror back to them a confining or demeaning or contemptible picture of themselves. Nonrecognition or misrecognition can both inflict harm and be a form of oppression, imprisoning someone in a false, distorted, and reduced mode of being."[5]

Even though national identities can be homogenizing and monolithic, the mediation of inclusion and the accommodation of difference can remove the walls of distinctions dividing people by race, creed, and color—as if two epistemologies, Native American and European, shared a library, thus giving hope that cultural diversity and multiculturalism, the currency of globalization, will eventually bridge the gap between recognition and identity.

Artists such as Tsinhnahjinnie and Heap of Birds have created their spaces of identity despite the vitriolic culture of poverty, homelessness, landlessness, and hopelessness. Tsinhnahjinnie's platinum Lambda print *Hoke-tee* (2003), from a series of ten portraits known as *Portraits Against Amnesia*, transports a young girl from the earth to the moon through the portal of digital technology. The artist visualizes a man going to the moon and trying to claim it, only to discover a little aboriginal baby floating above the surface of the moon on her space scooter.[6]

Native American artists, against great odds, have continued to flourish and endure. We find new markets for our work, and we contribute to finding new ways of defining who we are, continuing to make art for family, community, ceremony, and ritual. Creative spaces of Native cultural identity inside the world's only superpower are significant in their resilience. The forceful sociopolitical spaces of conceptual artist Heap of Birds, for example, are achieved through language trajectories installed in public places, such as his *Wheel* (2005) at the Denver Art Museum in Colorado. He has designed an outdoor sculpture inspired by traditional Native medicine wheels for the front of the museum. With its proximity to the museum, *Wheel* has a healing power and has initiated new exchanges of ideas. Heap of Birds writes in *Blasted Allegories*:

> For we the Tsistsistas people to be able to continue our native life, we have formed two survival tactics used simultaneously for our precious preservation. The sickening fact of the United States of America hunting down and murdering our women, children and warriors is still fresh in our minds. The quiet plan of self-imposed isolation from the white man has brought us to this day–living people, thus escaping the brutal swords and gunfire. As a second and less popular tactic, we find it

effective to challenge the white man through our use of the mass media. As in American business and culture, in order to survive one must communicate a mass appeal. [7]

The idea of including Native American history and culture in the national culture has been made real through the creation of the Smithsonian's National Museum of the American Indian, first in New York City and now in Washington, D.C. This recognition is an important initiative by the United States to include first Americans in its nation building. Now, it is up to Native people to claim, articulate, and share our ideas and assume the complex responsibilities of a major cultural institution with its own genetic code. The unpredictable mutation of the evolving canon of Western modern art is not a formless multiplicity, but rather a manifestation of multiple modernities in which Native America can be examined.

First Nations Saulteaux artist Robert Houle is also a curator, teacher, and writer. He currently lives and works in Toronto, Ontario, Canada.

NOTES

1. Steven Newcomb and Birgil Kills Straight, "The Legacy of Fifteenth-Century Papal Bulls and Indigenous Nations and Peoples." Paper prepared for the 2005 UN Permanent Forum on Indigenous Issues panel, Challenging the Doctrine of Discovery, Christianity, Papal Bulls and Manifest Destiny, May 2005.

2. Robert Houle, "The Emergence of a New Aesthetic Tradition," in *New Works by a New Generation* (Regina, Norman Mackenzie Art Gallery: 1982), 3.

3. Houle, "Kay WalkingStick," in *Land Spirit Power: First Nations at the National Gallery of Canada* (Ottawa, National Gallery of Canada: 1922), 214.

4. W. Jackson Rushing, "What the Ground Says: The Art of James Lavadour," in *Into the Fray: The Eiteljorg Fellowship for Native American Fine Art, 2005* (Indianapolis, Eiteljorg Museum of American Indians and Western Art: 2005), 80.

5. Charles Taylor, *Multiculturalism and the "Politics of Recognition,"* ed. Amy Gutmann (Boston, Princeton University Press: 1992), 25.

6. Veronica Passalacqua, "Hulleah Tsinhnahjinnie," in *Path Breakers: The Eiteljorg Fellowship for Native American Fine Art, 2003* (Indianapolis, Eiteljorg Museum of American Indians and Western Art: 2003), 96.

7. Edgar Heap of Birds, "Sharp Rocks," in *Blasted Allegories: An Anthology of Artists' Writings,* ed. Brian Wallis (New York, The New Museum of Contemporary Art: 1987), 170.

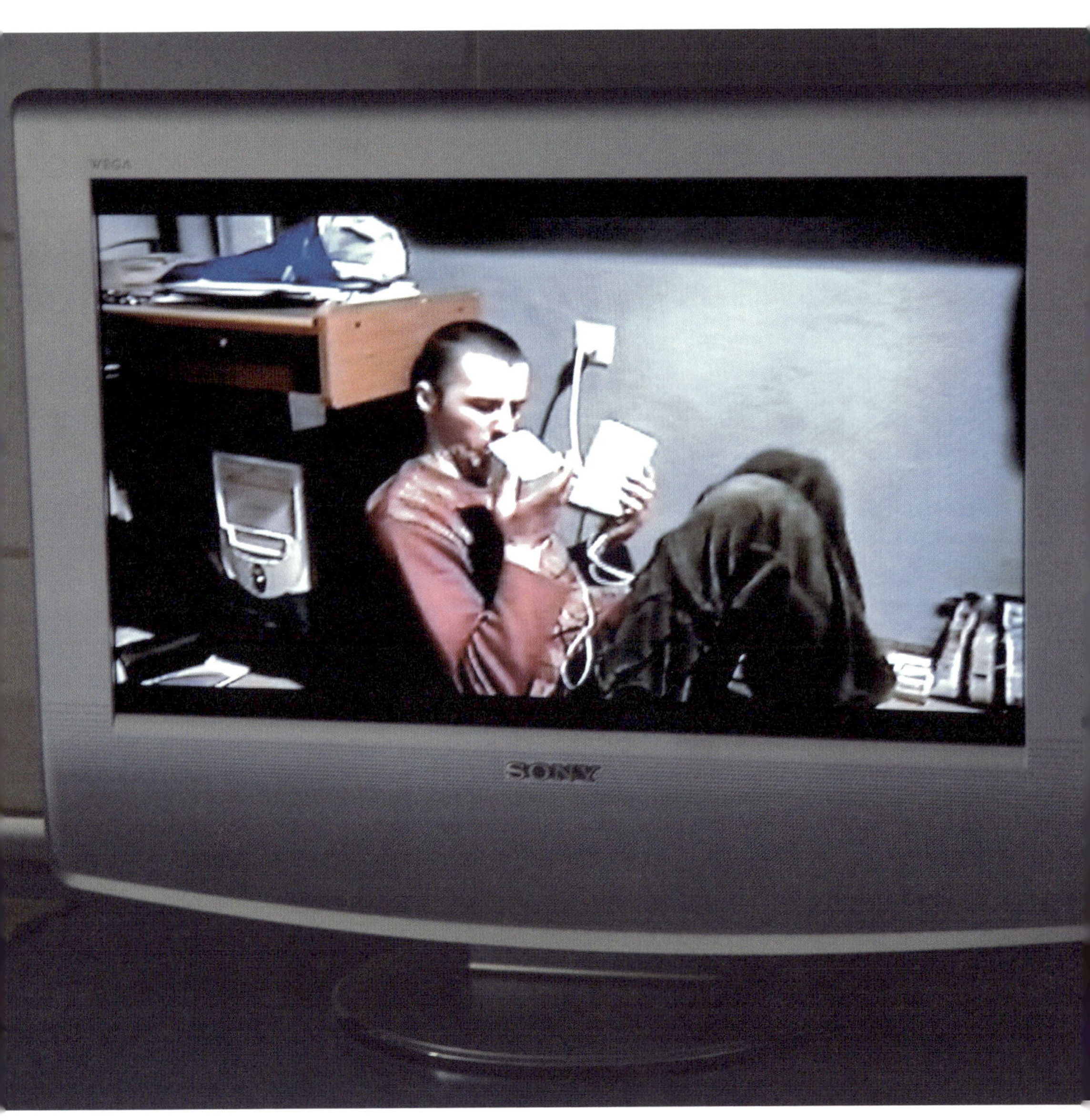

VASIF KORTUN

Doing the Homework

People ask me about my next big project, but, after the Istanbul Biennial, I do not have a large project planned. I stress this because I do not think it is necessary to go from project to project and scan the whole globe. If the Biennial was originally planned as a way for Istanbul to "catch up" on the development of visual culture in the United States, the original European Union, and Japan, then that has been accomplished. Now, Istanbul can stand on its own terms, as a crucial fulcrum of social and cultural change and a place that can inspire outsiders to new perspectives and extraordinary new work.

I want to summarize a few experiences from the past fifteen years and then talk about a few projects from the 9th International Istanbul Biennial (2005), which I think is appropriate in this context. My institution, Platform Garanti Contemporary Art Center, last year featured *Normalization,* a series of four exhibitions on the issue of normalization. The theme references not only Turkey's transition from a national economy to a neo-liberal one but also other forms of so-called normalization taking place in Eastern Europe and the dissolving of the welfare state. The exhibition asked such questions as: Who gets normalized? What are the processes of normalization? Who benefits from it?

Jakup Ferri (Prishtina, Kosovo, b. 1981), *Three Virgins,* 2003. Video – DVD, 6:20 min. © Jakup Ferri.

Creating a New Condition

In 1989, I invited Homi Bhabha to Istanbul for a lecture. I asked for the support of the British Council, and they replied by saying that he would not be good enough for Turkey. You can imagine that in those days not only were institutions like the British Council based on packing and traveling art that they found appropriate from their homes to abroad, they were not likely to engage in discussions requested from the locals on the ground. I relate this anecdote to help convey the context of the time, just prior to the watershed events of 1989.

In 1990, I traveled in Germany with a number of artist files. Young and eager, I sought to find venues for artists from Turkey in exhibitions and to increase awareness of their art. I went to the Institut für Auslandsbeziehungen, whose mission was to support this type of endeavor. This federal institution helps exhibitions from abroad come to Germany and vice-versa.

They did not let me in the door. No appointment, no nothing, left outside without even a coffee. And so I returned. On the train back from Stuttgart, I had an epiphany—a great feeling. Never, ever export again, I thought. I am just going to go back home and do the homework. I will go home and produce a condition where you know things will eventually turn out right. And this is what I have been doing for the last fourteen years or so like many others from the so-called peripheries of the old and new world. In 1992, we held the 3rd International Istanbul Biennial. Canada was part of this show, with Bruce Ferguson as curator of that section.

Around that time, the Soros Centers, the Open Society Institutes, were founded, mostly for Eastern Europe and the former Soviet Republics. A network called Soros Centers for Contemporary Art (SCCA) was part of the Open Society initiative there. I was extremely positive about the SCCA network because this was an occasion, finally, for a regional conversation, a region-to-region, horizontal conversation. Actually, it did not happen that way. Many artists wanted to go to New York or to Sao Paulo. I remember there were some seventy artists from the former Eastern Block in San Paulo in 1994. They let me crash in. That was a lost opportunity, but things are much better now. Perhaps most Soros Centers for Contemporary Art closed because they were still carrying in part the former operating habits of official socialism—the old *nomenclatura* of the Soviet Union—or these places were found to be simply "normalized." But now the younger artists in Turkey are looking to Kosovo or Beirut. They are not looking to New York anymore—in fact, nobody is looking at New York, which is the emptied-out center.

In conversations over the last few days, a lot of fuss was made about using English while we are in Italy at an international conference. It brings to mind a 1993 work by Croatian artist Mladen Stilinovic titled *An Artist Who Cannot Speak English Is No Artist.* Made of acrylic on artificial silk and 140 by 240 centimeters in size, this is a beautiful piece; it is also a banner for the streets and a kind of demonstration. The artwork indicates ambivalence about criticizing the place one is from as well as the operatives of the ever-globalizing art world. English is a common communication interface that we bend, warp, transform, and make our own. The empire may have been extended but at the same time lost its center.

Artists at the 2005 Istanbul Biennial

In the 9th International Istanbul Biennial (2005), we showed a video work by Kosovar artist Jakup Ferri in which he takes Stilinovic's concept to the extreme by trying to communicate through words he does not know the meaning of. You have to realize that Kosovo is under very special conditions right now. After the breakup of Yugoslavia and eruption of ethnic strife, the UN stepped in and took over control of Kosovo in 2001. Still, it has great institutions, a good school, and a very interesting group of young artists and writers. Ferri makes very short videos about being an artist in Kosovo or being an artist in Eastern Europe. In a work called *Save Me, Help Me,* he actually displays art as if in the marketplace—he sits down waiting for the European curator or collector who will, he hopes, someday arrive. In a video-performance work titled *Three Virgins,* Ferri plays an album track in which John Lennon and Yoko Ono display their affection for one another in an orgasmic counterpoint of whispers and shouts that grows ever more frantic. Hiding like a teenager in his room, hugging cheap computer speakers close to his heart, Ferri tries to insert himself in the main narrative, saying over and over: "Jakup, Jakup." It is a memorable piece.

In another video work, Ferri puts his parents and sisters in front of the camera in a comic exploration of the artist's emergence into the Western art world. Ferri is participating for the first time in an exhibition curated by René Block, who has a sense of amazing hospitality and generosity. Ferri's father begins by expressing gratitude to the curator, but he lets us know that he holds his son's paintings in more esteem than the videos that have been selected for the show. Then the mother takes her turn and warns Jakup against the evils of the West, as in a video letter. But the whole thing breaks down because one of Jakup's sisters collapses in tears—she is laughing so hard that she begins to cry. The entire piece is actually a kind of setup. Ferri is in complete apprehension of his position as an artist from the extreme periphery of Europe and by playing the naive role pulls a royal flush on us. The three young women who form the Istanbul-based artist group Oda Projesi worked for the last seven years from a small apartment in a distressed part of town where they transformed the protocols of guest and host, audience and community, as well as hierarchy. They published a book for the 2005 Istanbul Biennial titled *Neighbourhood, room, neighbour, guest?* Focusing on people's relations to their situations and social environments, the book is a symbolic conversation among people who have experienced Oda Projesi yet do not know each other. It is based on questions that Oda Projesi has asked, such as: What kind of changes have you seen in your neighborhood since you came in? Did you do anything to your neighborhood? What does it mean to be a neighbor? What kind of neighbor are you? The questions led to other questions from participants and a conversation. More than 150 people from different walks of life and geographical locations were involved in an interactive network—you would have a nine-year-old in a conversation with an urbanist from Germany. It is an achronological, democratic book in which you can start with any question on any page, and the questions and answers will take you in any direction you want to go.

The whole story of Oda Projesi indicates that they were always guests. They almost never ever made "exhibitions." Audience was merely a surplus. You could happily go to the apartment, but you did not necessarily have to go there because things were already taking place with or without you. In effect, there was no community either. I think art can actually help make concrete, palpable change if it persists in this mode.

Vasif Kortun is the Director of Platform Garanti Contemporary Art Center in Istanbul, Turkey. He co-curated the 9th International Istanbul Biennial in 2005.

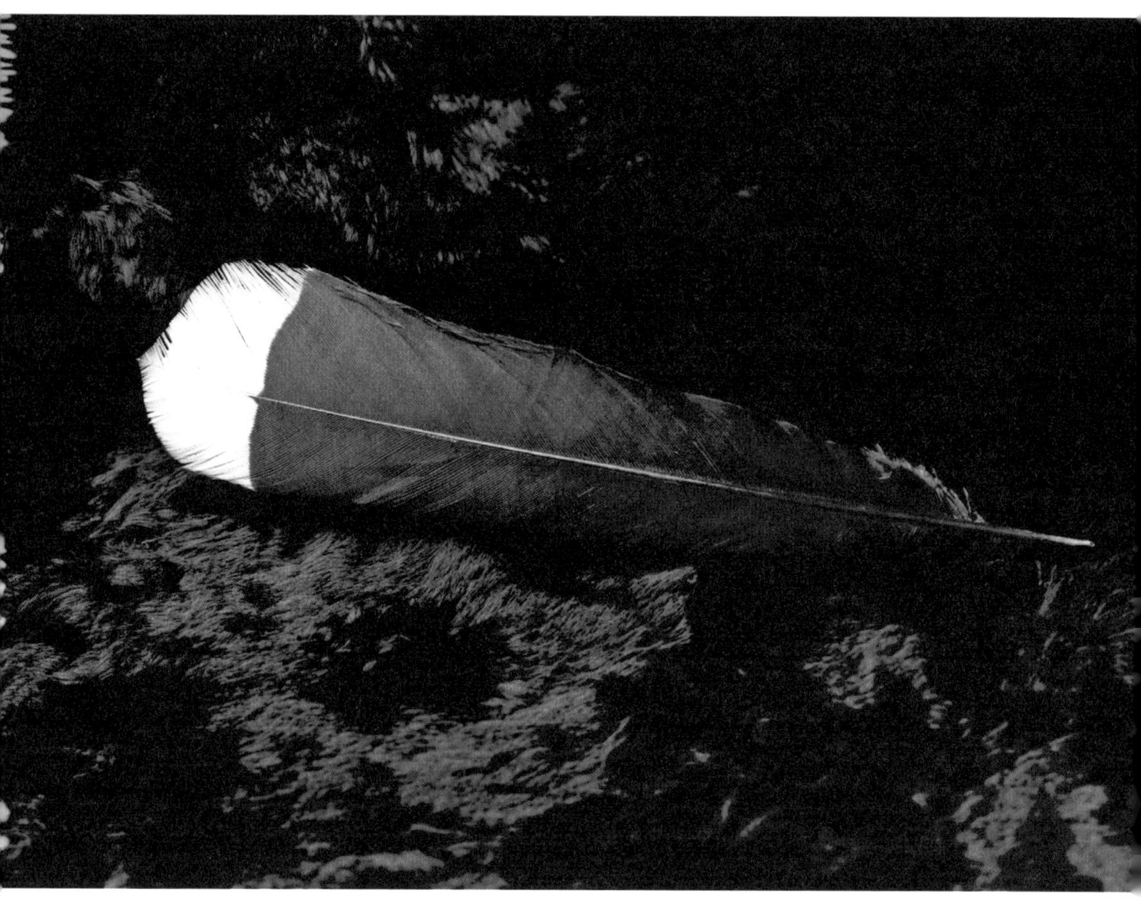

Fiona Pardington (Kai Tahu, Kati Mamoe, b. 1961), *Te huia tu rae/The huia that sits on my brow*, 2002. Silver gelatin photograph. © Fiona Pardington.

MEGAN TAMATI-QUENNELL

Te Aö Täwhiti, Te Aö Hou—Old Worlds, New Worlds

Kö Ranginui kei rünga
Kö Papatuanüku kei raro
Kö ngä tängata kei waenganui
Tihei mauri ora.

Kei te mihi ahau i te Mätua nui i te rangi, nana nei ngä mea katoa
E ngä kärangaranga maha
E te whänau whänui, e te iwi whänui
Tena koutou
Tena koutou
Tena koutou kätoa.

Kö Te Atiawa raua kö Ngäi Tahu öku iwi
Kö Raniera Erihana raua kö Hana Nikuru Weller öku tüpuna
Nö Te Wähi Pounamu töku ükaipo
Kö Megan Tamati-Quennell taku ingoa.

The greeting I gave is a brief *mihi* in my own language to acknowledge my place in the world, to thank the people who invited me to participate in the National Museum of the American Indian's symposium, *Vision, Space, Desire: Global Perspectives and Cultural Hybridity,* and to introduce myself. Translated it says:

To the Sky Father above
To the Earth Mother below
To the people who exist between
There is life.

Greetings to the creator of all things
Calls of welcome
To all humanity, to all people
Greetings to everyone here.

I am of the Te Atiawa and Ngäi Tahu people of New Zealand
A grandchild of Raniera Erihana and Hana Nikuru Weller
Born of the place of greenstone, the land of the South Island of New Zealand
My name is Megan Tamati-Quennell.

I want not only to address the idea of "Performing Cultural Hybridity" established for this session of the symposium but also to demonstrate it through a project, *Te Aö Täwhiti, Te Aö Hou—Old Worlds, New Worlds,* that I developed as an independent curator. I will also outline the project's context—the position of contemporary Mäori art in New Zealand.

Since arriving in Venice and attending Robert Storr's International Biennale Symposium *Where Art Worlds Meet: Multiple Modernities and the Global Salon* that dovetails with *Vision, Space, Desire,* I have expanded my paper to pick up on an idea expressed by Gerardo Mosquera, adjunct curator at the New Museum of Contemporary Art in New York, in the session "One, Two, Many Biennials: How Do Local Conditions Prompt and Shape the Spread of the Global Salon?" I have reframed my paper to incorporate Mosquera's notion of "creating our own space, our own values, and projecting those into the world."

Mosquera's approach is one I have used regularly in my own curatorial practice and one that appeals to my Guerrilla Girl, subversive tendencies. Employing it in my curatorial practice means you can change the balance, reverse the position and the gaze. It enables you to frame projects from the inside out, move from the margins to the center within the art mainstream, and invite others into reworked and retranslated spaces; as Mosquera says, a form of "revolution, with fun." It is also an approach that could be deemed as inherent within Māori culture, one that expresses our contemporary dynamism, continuing evolution and innovation, and the culture's fluidity. An historical example of this relates to a *whakapapa* or genealogy constructed for New Zealand Europeans a century after Captain Cook, one of the European founders, first anchored off New Zealand in October 1769.

For Māori, the fabric that held the knowledge of the world together was whakapapa (genealogy). As Rawiri Te Maire Tau observes, "Every 'thing' was related and all 'things' we held together by genealogical connections that eventually referenced back to the self."[1] And in her essay "Identity: Moving Beyond Colonial Impositions," Leonie Pihema writes:

Whakapapa is a powerful notion that expresses the complex set of interrelationships we have—*whanau, hapu,* and *iwi* (family, sub-tribe, and tribe)—but contrary to popular belief does not deny us as individuals, rather what it argues for is the prioritising of cultural relationships over a notion of privileging the individual.... Identity is neither fixed nor closed but is a system of complex shifts, positions, relationships and interrelationships. All Maori people have whakapapa. Not having knowledge of whakapapa may render it invisible; however, it does not negate its existence. Whakapapa remains irrespective of our knowledge of it. Our Tūpunā will always be our Tūpunā (our ancestors always our ancestors).[2]

The whakapapa constructed for New Zealand Europeans starts with the Māori ātua or God Takaroa, God of the sea, and Papatuanuku, Earth Mother, and ends with Kiwa, associated with Te Mōananui ā Kiwa, the great ocean of Kiwa from where in a literal sense Europeans did come—out of the Ocean, out of the sea—highlighting how whakapapa, a Māori knowledge system and frame of reference, was expanded to include the other and the unknown.

Contemporary Mäori art itself, a relatively new phenomenon, can be related to as "Performing Cultural Hybridity." It can also be defined, using Mosquera's concept, as an assertion of our own space and a representation of our values and pushing those out into the world—although the artists and their new styles, materials, and techniques were not always supported by the Elders. Many Elders held a retrenched position and worried that the introduction of "nontraditional" expression and material would harm the culture. As Brett Graham, artist and son of Mäori artist Fred Graham, told me: "With Dad's group there was a lot more tension because those ones …were seen as changing or bastardising Mäori art."[3]

Mäori Modernists

Mäori artists Fred Graham, Ralph Hotere, Selwyn Wilson, Katerina Mataira, Cath Brown, Muru Walters, Paratene Matchitt, and others known as the Mäori modernists have been described as the first generation of Mäori artists to engage with the styles, materials, and techniques of modern European art, especially the work of Picasso, Brancusi, Barbara Hepworth, and Henry Moore. They held the first group exhibition of contemporary Mäori art in Auckland in 1958 and exhibited work in 1963 at the first Mäori Festival of the Arts held at Türangawaewae in Ngäruawähia, Waikato, in the central region of the North Island of New Zealand.

The development of new creative directions in Mäori art, begun in the late 1950s, gained momentum in the '70s. The New Zealand Mäori Artists and Writers Society was founded in 1973. After the introduction of the Treaty of Waitangi Act in 1975 (legislation to provide for the observance and confirmation of the principles of the Treaty, the founding document of New Zealand), contemporary Mäori art reflected our developing politicization and discontent with our lack of power, landlessness, cultural alienation, and marginal status in relation to the dominant Pakeha (European New Zealand) culture. Many contemporary Mäori artists of the '70s and '80s (and into the '90s) used their art as an influential force in the resurgence of Mäori nationalism and culture. Many used their work to create political statements about social justice. John Bevan Ford states about contemporary Mäori art:

> The birth of the New Zealand Mäori Artists and Writers Society in 1973 was an act of self-assertion. All the artists…represent the pioneers of a new consciousness, single warriors in a battle for new creative directions, who came together to support each other at a time of cultural insecurity.
>
> The Mäori artist of yesterday created within the constraints of a single culture. Now the Mäori artist operates within a multiplicity of cultures.
>
> The creative process includes the invention of new symbols, which denote the dilemma of a people who were once the only people of the land but are now just a part of the total.[4]

Te Mäori, an exhibition of *täonga,* Maori cultural treasures (customary Mäori art) opened at the Metropolitan Museum of Art in New York in 1984 and became a watershed exhibition and turning point for Mäori art. Although it did not appear to engage with ideas of cultural hybridity or a way to create our own space, *Te Mäori* caused a paradigm shift that radically transformed New Zealand museum and art gallery practices and changed the way Mäori art was seen in New Zealand. *Te Mäori* moved täonga out of the ethnographic frame it had been locked within and repositioned it for the first time as art, a concept imported into the culture after colonization. Sid Mead wrote of *Te Mäori:*

> I saw the redefinition of *taonga whakairo* (Mäori carvings) happen in New York in a most dramatic way. Maori art was transformed and in a sense "released" and "freed" from the history and intellectual context in which our artworks had been "imprisoned." I saw our *taonga* (customary Mäori art) become art by destination.…
>
> This was one context. Another was to take Maori art out of a New Zealand context of misty obscurity and thrust it onto the world stage of international art.[5]

Te Māori Te Hōkingā Mai, as the exhibition was called when it returned home and toured New Zealand in 1986, not only opened the way for a more open and respectful understanding of customary Māori art and culture, inside and out of museums, but it also instigated the development of a strong and recognized contemporary Māori art practice within the mainstream art world, thirty years after the first attempts of the late '50s and '60s to shift the ground.

Mainstream art galleries, including the then National Art Gallery in Wellington, started collecting contemporary Māori art seriously in the mid '80s and New Zealand art history began to regard it as an important and developing art movement, unique to Aōtearoa (New Zealand). In the '90s, contemporary Māori art gained further acceptance within the art mainstream as artists like Jacqueline Fraser, Peter Robinson, Shane Cotton, Brett Graham, Lisa Reihana and Michael Parekowhai gained credence for their work and practice nationally, and status and recognition as "Māori internationals" with global opportunity. In *Taiawhio: Conversations with Contemporary Māori Artists,* artist Emily Karaka notes:

> Our culture has grown and grown; I don't believe it is static…it is timeless knowledge, so it belongs in the past, the present and the future, so it must have the capacity to move. I think it is coming out of those dark ages. There have been two elements used to contain it— fear and cultural conceit—getting out of those is where it is at.[6]

Despite such progress, contemporary Māori art and culture are still often misrepresented, marginalized, and misunderstood. Non-Māori—and even some Māori—curators continue to work with assumptions about culture and ethnicity, often accompanied by a clichéd bicultural logic that fails to provide full readings of the work and intentions of contemporary Māori artists. Jacqueline Fraser, who along with fellow Ngāi Tahu artist Peter Robinson represented New Zealand in our inaugural exhibition at the Venice Biennale in 2001, although staunchly of the Ngāi Tahu tribe, now resists the classification of "Māori artist" because it limits understanding of her work and the many contexts she addresses. She even stopped showing in New Zealand, at one stage dropping her two New Zealand dealers and working with a dealer in Sydney, Australia, and New York in an effort to become more international. Internationally, contemporary Māori art hardly even registers. Much of the international exposure and advance has been attained not through government support and effort but from the individual strength and creative vision of single artists who, like Fraser and Robinson (and earlier like Ralph Hotere in the mid '60s), have created their own paths. It could be argued that New Zealand's representation at the 2001 Venice Biennale featuring the work of Robinson and Fraser, a never-repeated occurrence, remains the highest-profile, nationally endorsed international exhibition of contemporary Māori art.

The inclusion of two suites of photographic works—one by Ngāi Tahu artist Fiona Pardington and one by Ngā-Ariki, Te Aitanga-ā-Mahaki, and Rongowhakaata artist Michael Parekowhai—in the opening program, June 2006, of the Musée du Quai Branly, the new museum in Paris dedicated to Africa, Asia, Oceania, and the Americas, is the most recent significant international presence of contemporary Māori art that gained some national support. A proposed international tour of a major contemporary Māori art exhibition of the magnitude of *Te Māori* to "take Māori art out of a New Zealand context of misty obscurity and thrust it onto the world stage of international art" and highlight the movement as the creative and dynamic force it is, has yet to gain the necessary national support and recognition.

Virtual Space

Te Aō Tāwhiti, Te Aō Hou—Old Worlds, New Worlds, like Māori people and culture post-colonization, deals with ideas of the constructed, the changing, and the redefinition of the self and world. It is part of a CD-ROM project developed for *Artpix 3: Aotearoa/New Zealand* and was produced by a non-profit organization based in Houston, Texas, and run by art independents Fredericka Hunter and Ian Glennie. *Te Aō Tāwhiti, Te Aō Hou—Old Worlds, New Worlds* was one of four projects created for the CD-ROM that was to be a sampling and representation of current practice and thinking in the field of contemporary New Zealand art.

Te Aö Täwhiti, Te Aö Hou—Old Worlds, New Worlds presents the invented worlds of artists Lisa Reihana and John Pule. Both created worlds of Polynesian spirit that viewers can enter and experience. John Pule's *Born in Paradise* is a narrated and illustrated prose poem adapted from the prologue of his first novel, *The Shark That Ate the Sun.* Constructed of dream, memory, magic, and history, Pule's world speaks of migration, dislocation, settlement, family ties, anti-nuclear protest, anti-colonialism, violence, and desire. Lisa Reihana's *Fluffy Fings,* inspired by the underwater magic of an aquarium and the cultural diaspora, the migration of Pacific and Mäori peoples to Australia, is a video work of the installation of the same name that she created for the Sydney Pacific Wave Festival in 1998. Shot in the style of Jacques Cousteau, Reihana's video offers a swim through a dreamscape, seascape, and underwater fantasia fish tank of brilliantly colored hybrid, tactile creatures fashioned from feathers, fibers, glass, and animal horns.

Both indigenous and both with the advantage of being at once inside and outside of their respective cultures, Pule and Reihana operate simultaneously in dual worlds and create imagery that is uniquely their own. Drawing from local and global, past and present, real and imaginary, they create work that is related and relevant in essence to their ethnicity but not derived directly from their individual cultural heritages.

Originally from Liku, Niue, in Polynesia, John Pule writes and paints in a personal style. His work is linked to his birthplace, the land, and his ancestry of Niue, but also speaks of his experience as a Niuean immigrant in New Zealand—of being a person in another's land. He creates his own image-filled stories, symbols, and iconography; some forms are drawn loosely from traditional narratives, including the patterns of Niuean *hiäpö*/bark cloth, while others are derived from incidents and events in his own life.

Lisa Reihana is from the northern part of the North Island of New Zealand and is of Ngä Pühi, Ngäti Hine, and Ngäi Tü Mäori descent. A weaver of image and story in fiber, film, and new media, Reihana creates art that relates to her experience as an urban Mäori. Her artworks, which give voice to contemporary city culture, are her interpretation of traditional concepts and art forms and are touchstones to deeper Mäori beliefs and ideas.

Based on my experience with the *Artpix 3* project, new media seems to be a space we can make our own—a space able to expand and accommodate indigenous values and ideas. In addition to *Te Aö Täwhiti, Te Aö Hou—Old Worlds, New Worlds,* I was asked to create the frame for the *Artpix 3* project— the context in which contemporary New Zealand art would be positioned and read from. Using language and song, I created a virtual ritual space and a *pöwhiri* (a Mäori ceremony of encounter) as the mechanism for engaging with the works contained within. The virtual pöwhiri consisted of a contemporary *Käranga, mihi,* and *waiata* (call of welcome, greeting, and song), and the project was completed with a *poroporoäki,* farewell. The framing recontextualized the project, was a representation of a Mäori space and values, and, like the whakapapa/geneaology written at the turn of the century for New Zealand Europeans, demonstrated how a Mäori construct could be expanded to include both the other and the unknown and could be the position from which we project our culture and art into the world.

Megan Tamati-Quennell (Te Atiäwä/Ngäi Tahu/Käti Mamoe) is Curator of Contemporary Mäori and Indigenous Art at the Museum of New Zealand Te Papa Tongarewa, Wellington.

NOTES

1. Rawiri Te Maire Tau, "The Death of Knowledge, Ghosts on the Plains," *The New Zealand Journal of History* 35, no. 2 (October 2001): 131–52.

2. Leonie Pihama, "Identity: Moving Beyond Colonial Impositions," in *The Nervous System: Twelve Artists Explore Images and Identities in Crisis* (Wellington: City Art Gallery, 1995), 20–27.

3. Personal conversation with the author, 2004.

4. John Bevan Ford, "Introduction," in Katarina Mataira, *Mäori Artists of the South Pacific* (Raglan, NZ: New Zealand Artists & Writers Society, 1984), 9.

5. Sidney Moko Mead, "Concepts and Models for Maori Museums and Cultural Centres," *AGMANZ Journal* 16, no. 3 (September 1985): 2–5.

6. Emily Karaka in conversation with Megan Tamati-Quennell, in Huhana Smith, ed., *Taiäwhiö: Conversations with Contemporary Mäori artists* (Wellington: Te Papa Press, 2002), 88–97.

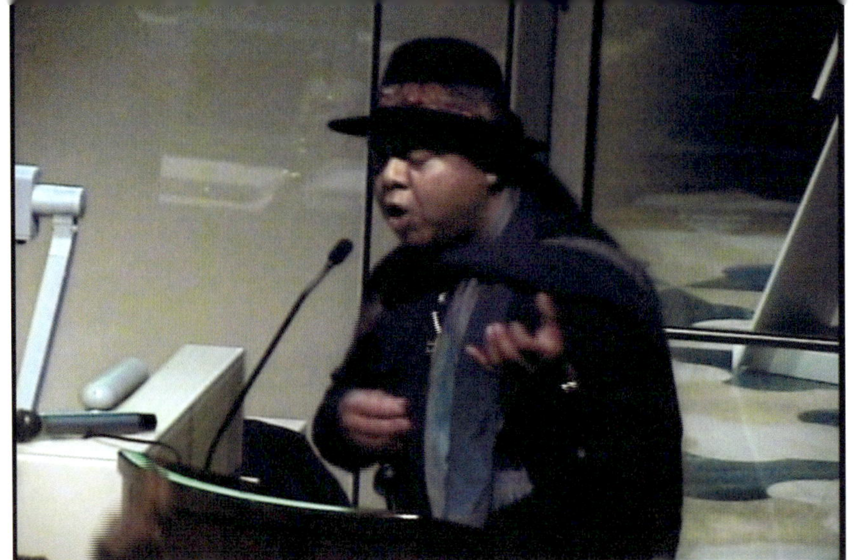

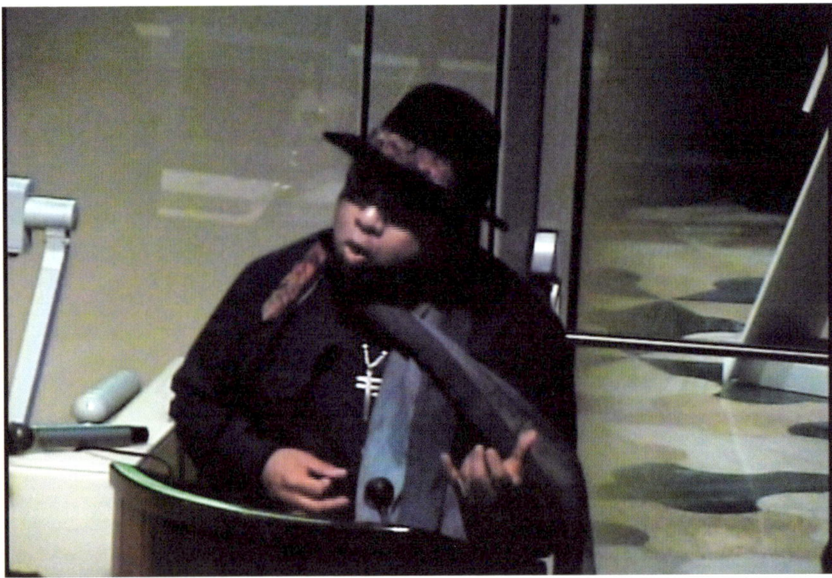

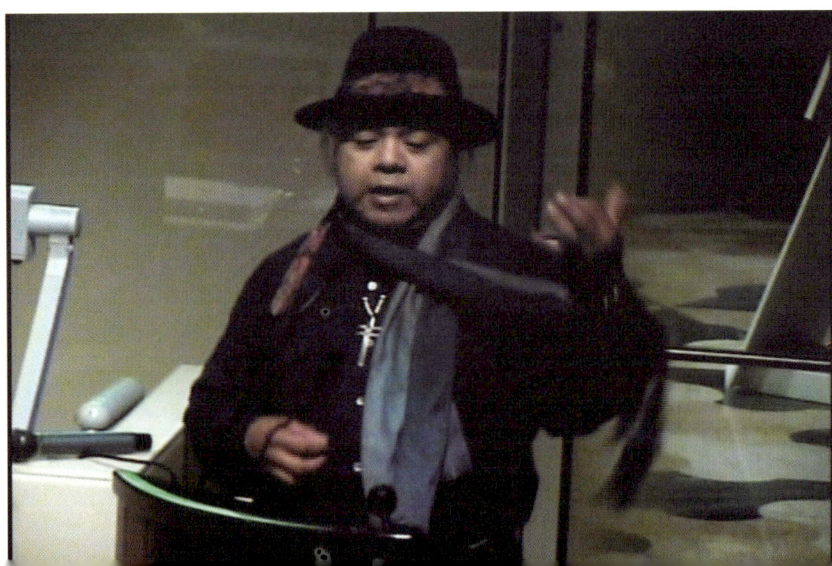

JAMES LUNA

Excuse Me While I Kiss the Sky

I am very pleased, of course, to see Native people at the symposium. But as an educator, I am even more pleased to see non-Native people here. Whenever we had a multicultural event about school issues, it was primarily populated by multicultural people. I know why we go, but I wondered why these events were not attended by the people who were going to make the difference—the ninety new people that made up the school boards, the principals, and most of the teachers. So I thank you for your patience and understanding and being here with us.

I am going to need your help here. Would you please stand? I am going to need a little beat. Yeah. Hold it. Keep going. Maybe a little harder.

[After getting the audience to stand and clap their hands, Luna takes off his tie and transforms it into a band for a hat that he pulls out of his bag. He puts on the hat and adds a pair of sunglasses to the costume. Luna then hums the music of Jimi Hendrix's "Purple Haze" and pretends to play an electric guitar. After a brief moment of playing, he motions for the audience to take their seats and begins to speak.]

Grazie. Crossing the waters in 1966, Jimi Hendrix arrived in London from the United States. He came to be discovered. After years of frustration, living on a shoestring, playing lowlife gigs throughout the country from Seat-

James Luna (Luiseño), presentation at the National Museum of the American Indian's symposium *Vision, Space, Desire: Global Perspectives and Cultural Hybridity*, Venice, Italy, December 13, 2005. Stills from digital video by Istituto Veneto di Scienze, Lettere ed Arti. © NMAI.

tle to the Chitlin' Circuit in the South to the East Coast, he came to England to be discovered. Chas Chandler of the The Animals saw him and understood that he fit a niche, but that it would not happen in America—in America he was a little bit much. Hendrix came to England because he fit the niche of a black man playing blues-based rock 'n' roll rather than the trend of white guys playing their version of the blues. In a matter of months, he caught the eye of the clubs and the public. They labeled him "The Wild Man from Borneo," not knowing quite what to do with him.

In 1834, a Luiseño Indian named Pablo Tac (1822–1841) was brought by Father Antonio Peyri from a small village on the coast of what is now north San Diego County in California to Rome, Italy. He came to be trained as a missionary; one of many indigenous people chosen to come with the idea that they would return to their lands and spread the word of Jesus to their fellow heathens. I can imagine him being in awe, as I would have been, of the art, music, and literature—the culture of Western civilization found in Rome. He came of his own free will, I believe, intent on becoming a scholar. And I think he grasped the importance of trying to preserve our culture because he saw the ramifications of European colonization. Perhaps it was a losing battle. But the least that he could do was to write it down. He produced the first grammar and partial dictionary of the Luiseño language, knowing full well that these documents would somehow preserve our culture that seemingly was doomed.

May 2005: James Luna arrives in Venice. It has been a long, hard road, but in 1987, in the right place at the right time, I got lucky—real lucky. Today, though, Mr. Luna remains an enigma in American art as one of the most famous and oldest emerging artists in contemporary art. After thirty years of work, can't say that he had a one-man show at an established institution. Can't say that his art is in major collections. He is misunderstood in many spaces and would be rejected by the turquoise circuit of Santa Fake and Scotts-tail. I can say that I am busy, and that is what I like. I can say that being challenged makes you tough; it makes you work harder, and I would like to think it shows in the work. Anyway, putting my hat back on, we are going back to Jimi.

Summer 1967, Jimi returns to America and blows their minds at the Monterey Pop Festival in front of the royalty of rock 'n' roll. In less than two years, he has come back as a guitar hero. But it is a long way from fame because when he is not performing and out in the street, he is perceived as some feminine looking, queer, nigger. The black community does not accept him because he plays white music and has white musicians in his band. But he perseveres and spends a year touring America trying to change minds, even taking a gig as the opening act for the pop group The Monkees.

He died (drugs were involved) in London in 1970. He was despondent at the time, tired from travel and money worries, only a short three years from that memorable date in Monterey. He never got to realize his dreams—one was to play with Miles Davis.

Pablo Tac was never to return home. He fell ill, died, and was buried in Rome. But he now lives on through his writings and words, a subject for a few enlightened scholars and this artist guy who said, "Write it down."

[After Luna says, "Write it down," he moves away from the podium, looks up, and shouts, "Tac. Tac. Tac. Tac." Pausing for a moment, he lets out his breath—one, two, three times—and on the fourth, lets it out slowly; this is the ending to a prayer in the Luiseño tradition. He continues with his talk.]

I returned to America on Wednesday, June 13, 2005, from the Venice Biennale. Having worked like never before in a short year, I was very happy to come home and see my mom, cook some beans, and have some tortillas and chili—real food. People on the Rez ask, "Hey, how was Venice?" Wanting to know more about the parties and such things because, like many lay people, they never did understand the art or Venice.

I received some press, but never made the Indian papers. But I did receive a compliment like no other when Marcia Vetroq wrote in the September issue of *Art in America,* Luna represented America. The phone has not been ringing off the hook because I came back, just like Jimi, to an America that had not changed. I know it is early, but I am no dummy. I came back disillusioned. I did not really like all that I saw here—the power, the money, the small controlling group that runs what we call the contemporary art world. And I thought about this, and I am still thinking about this. I have come to the conclusion that we should make our own space and let them catch up for once. I have heard words about inclusion and exclusion, but let's lead rather than be led. Let's put our money and our minds together, start out slow, and develop a place where we honor our artists. Artists, not artist. We can showcase our emerging artists and people that have been working for a long time and deserve recognition for their many accomplishments, as well as all the artists in between. It might happen in Canada, or it might happen in D.C., but I would like to see it happen in my lifetime.

I came back from Europe disillusioned, but there was no big illusion at the outset because I know that art is a business. If I came back with anything, it was that I may not be able to change this system, but, damn, it is not going to change me.

[Luna goes silent for a moment and then slowly looks up and raises his hand to the lights above.]

Excuse me while I kiss the sky.

Internationally recognized for his installation and performance art, James Luna (Luiseño) was selected by the National Museum of the American Indian to participate in the 2005 Venice Biennale with a work titled Emendatio. *He lives on the La Jolla Indian Reservation, San Diego County, California, and works as an academic counselor at Palomar College as well as teaching art part-time at the University of California, San Diego.*

Jaune Quick-to-See Smith (Enrolled Flathead Salish, Member of the Confederated Salish and Kootenai Nation of Montana, b. 1940), *Celebrate 40,000 Years of American Art*, 1995. Color collagraph, Sheet: 194.9 x 135.4 cm. Whitney Museum of American Art, New York; Purchase, with funds from The Horace W. Goldsmith Foundation (2000.191). © Jaune Quick-to-See Smith.

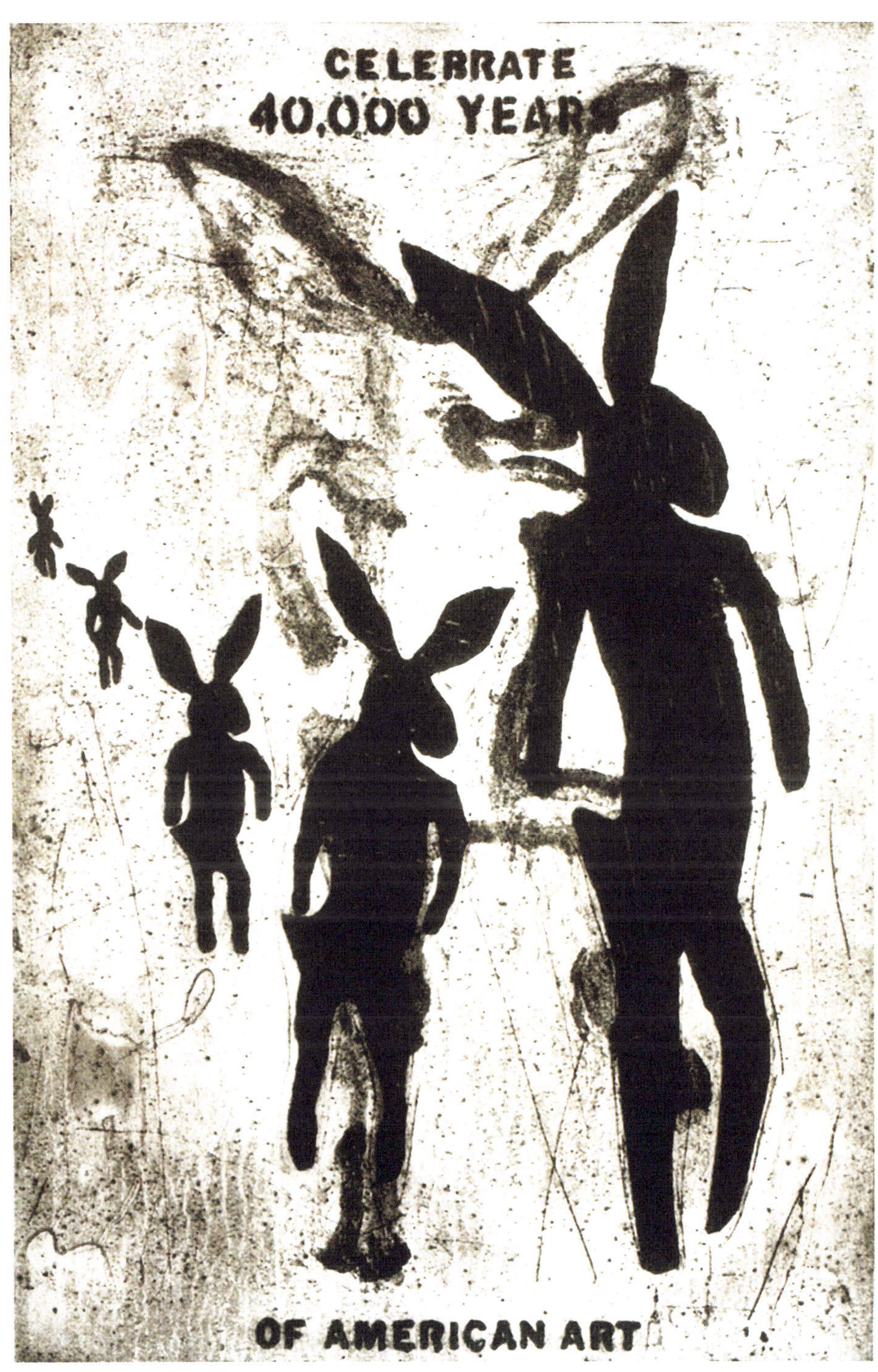
CELEBRATE
40,000 YEARS
OF AMERICAN ART

Rebecca Belmore (*Anishinabe*), *artist*

It was on the news. It was 1974. Indians with guns had taken over Anishinabe Park just outside of Kenora, Ontario, Canada. A pulp and paper mill had dumped mercury into the river system throughout the 1960s. In 1970, the federal government acknowledged the contamination and banned commercial fishing. This loss of livelihood affected the social condition of the First Nations communities tied to those waters. The armed occupation manifested the anger and frustration experienced by the people.

I recall my grandmother Maryanne watching her small, black-and-white, car-battery-operated television. She spoke, directing her Anishinabe words at the flickering screen. There was anger in her voice.

"Mom, what did Cocom just say?"

"She said, 'If I wasn't an old woman I would be there, too.'"

I looked at my grandmother. Imagined her with her hunting rifle in her hands. I looked at the screen and imagined her on TV.

I've been seen on television doing my art thing. Most recently, in Venice, as the "first Aboriginal woman" to place her work in the Canadian Pavilion at the 51st Venice Biennale. I had to deal constantly with the media trying to make me say something controversial and cope with the murmuring within the small Canadian art scene: "Do you think their choice was political?" Perhaps I was just paranoid—that little voice in my head. Cautious? Maybe.

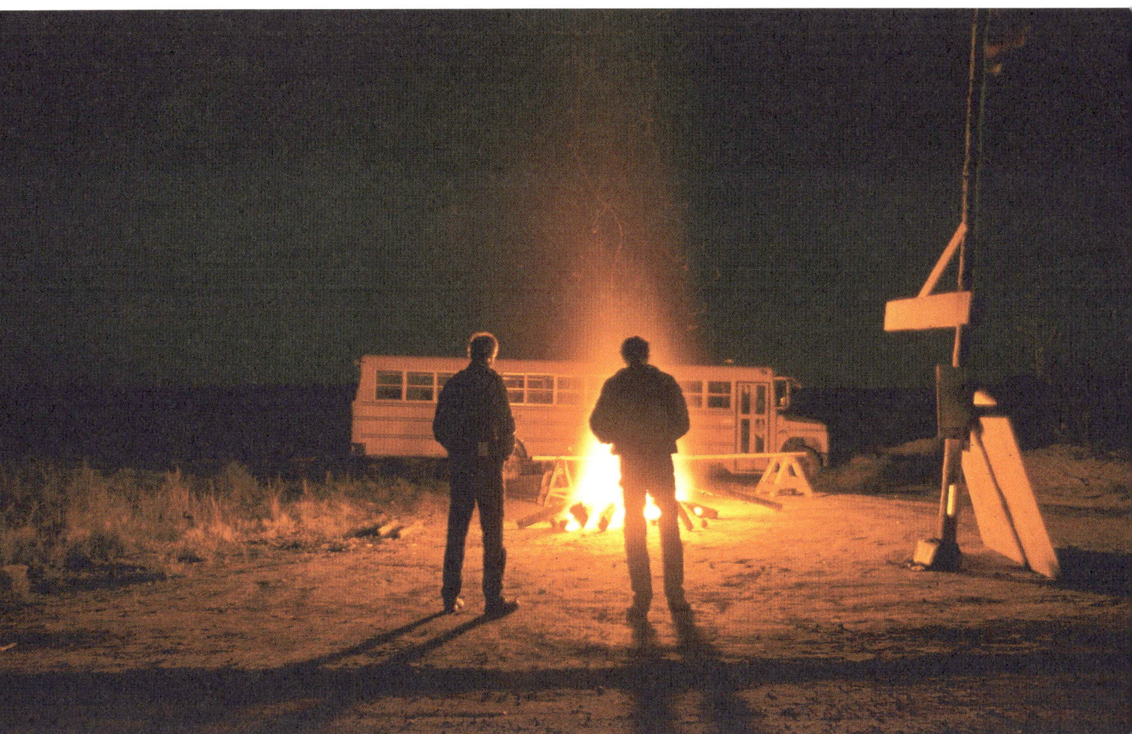

Logging blockade, north of Meadow Lake, Saskatchewan, Canada, 1992. Photo by Michael Beynon. © Rebecca Belmore.

Well, that ship has come and gone. Or was it a bus? Now, life is back to normal, and I feel like a passenger waiting to get back on. I have two strong images in my head that involve buses. One is of an evening sitting beside a bonfire with Cree people who were protesting the clear-cutting of land, north of Meadow Lake in Saskatchewan, late in the summer of 1992. They parked a big yellow school bus sideways to block a logging road. I remember thinking how beautiful the night was as we laughed and warmed ourselves with the flame, protected from the wind by the bus.

Someone else created the other image. I just happened to catch it on television. *Ipperwash: A Canadian Tragedy,* a documentary by Joan and John Goldi, told the story of the police shooting of Dudley George at Ipperwash Park in Southwestern Ontario in 1995. His death marked him as the first Aboriginal person in the twentieth century to be killed during a land claim dispute in this country. The scene I saw was a reenactment of an incident involving two teenage boys. They boarded an old school bus and furiously attempted to drive through the hatred that came at them that night. The boys were trying to rescue a protestor who was being beaten by the police riot squad. They were just children on a school bus fighting the police.

What is with Indians, public parks, and school buses in this country? Our parents, like all parents, dream of a better life for their children. The yellow bus is part of that dream. My childhood bus ride to school, partially on the highway but mostly dirt road, was almost an hour long. Back then, I was awed by the history of Columbus and imagined the *Niña*, the *Pinta*, and the *Santa Maria* bringing him and his men over here. I had yet to see an ocean.

In Venice, like so many tourists, I tried to picture what it must have been like to live there in its heyday. After a few weeks, I began to miss the feeling of solid ground beneath my feet. I was sent to Venice to present my work *Fountain*. I chose to use water and to throw blood. I made the work using the light of video projected onto a screen made of falling water.

Back home, I am still trying to sort out what that experience was for me. I think I drove my bus into history. What was the impact? I am not sure, but I am okay. I did my best to say something about us over there and them over here. It is a long ride, from the dirt roads of my early education to the historic shipbuilding city of Venice. I could never have imagined this journey, but I wish that my grandmother was still with us so she could have seen me on television, too.

ANNE ELLEGOOD, *Associate Curator, Hirshhorn Museum and Sculpture Garden*

An incomplete list of comments, thoughts, questions, and points of agreement and disagreement directly and indirectly related to two symposia in Venice in December 2005—*Where Art Worlds Meet* and *Vision, Space, Desire*—are offered here in no particular order.

After listening to the lively discussions taking place during five full days of panels, the most pronounced reaction I had, as a curator, was an increased awareness of the pressing need in contemporary art discourse and dialogue to consider and articulate the significant differences between various exhibition methodologies and venues for the presentation of art. The Biennale is very different from other frameworks/structures for viewing contemporary art. We are at a critical moment when the particular attributes, problems, and potentials of the biennale framework need to be distinguished from other platforms for viewing art. This need for distinction, in large part, made the dialogue at the symposia feel not only relevant but at times even urgent. It was reflected in comments by several participants, including Daniel Birnbaum, who expressed his concern that curators are being marginalized by the power of the art fairs, which strive to surpass a solely market-driven enterprise to become serious cultural events. Sylvie Fortin summed it up by saying that curatorial and artistic practices are being confused with market success and urged us to "unbind" these so that one is not equated with another. I appreciated Fortin's call for us to be precise with our language; in our discussions, we must distinguish between the practices, businesses, missions, and goals of museums, biennales, fairs, and galleries. There is no doubt that the current art market is having a large impact on the reception and understanding of art; it seems impossible to avoid conversations about the strength of the market and the inflated cost of works. Biennales may be the ideal umbrella under which some defiance of (or at least stepping back from) the marketplace is possible. A biennale is not a marketplace, it is not a site in which the valuation and exchange of works takes place openly. A biennale is not an art fair. Rather, these large-scale international exhibitions should be a platform to encourage and present work that has a more contested, even difficult relationship to the market. Biennales would feel more relevant and more meaningfully linked to their specific locales if they foregrounded the commissioning of art works so that artists and curators could spend real time in the city, allowing for genuine research and project development. (*InSite* is an important precedent here and an example to be studied.)

Many participants in the symposia agreed about the most pronounced problems of biennales. In considering how these issues might be addressed and in identifying what can be distinctive and successful about the biennale format, the suggestions and complaints of the artists spoke the loudest and should be seriously considered. Such valid concerns as lack of time to develop and create work, lack of real dialogue with the curator, substantial limitations to the kind of work that can be shown, failure to have any kind of discussion following the exhibition, lack of any kind of real risk-taking, concern that biennales are Eurocentric, failure to create platforms for artists to interact with other artists in the exhibition, and the problems of duplication and redundancy that accompany the mere fact of too many biennales taking place internationally each year, came up again and again.

When Salah Hassan quoted Franz Fanon's profound question, "Why does the other always have to talk about the other?" an awareness of how far we have to go to be truly inclusive (in academia, exhibition practice, criticism…in all areas) permeated the room. Hassan argued that the center/periphery dichotomy should be abandoned, a sentiment shared and expressed by many throughout the five days. His description of the world as multiple centers that are separate but linked provided a useful way of visualizing how local and global are intrinsically and increasingly related.

Accompanying the discussion of the need to still bridge the space between center and periphery was the matter of how biennales can be more inclusive of the work of indigenous people. Geeta Kapur was optimistic and inspirational on this topic by reminding us that biennales can create counternarratives and can have an enormous impact in communities where there are no major venues for the presentation of contemporary art. Salah Hassan and Paul Chaat Smith both discussed the desire and responsibility of curators to expand biennales to encompass the work of artists typically neglected, acknowledging the very real impact these exhibitions can have on an artist's career. Jolene Rickard argued that the invisibility of indigenous art must be fought through recognition and the integration of indigenous artists into the global conversation.

I found it surprising that Nancy Marie Mithlo's suggestion that we should work toward recognition of an indigenous aesthetic did not garner a heated discussion. She expressed the positive aspects of indigenous people looking toward their own knowledge and wisdom, and yet I was left wanting a clearer definition of what an indigenous aesthetic might mean, what it might actually look like. It strikes me as problematic to suggest that there may be a particular way for indigenous artists to work, or a particular aesthetic that would legitimate their work as authentic or meaningful. As someone in the audience pointed out, I think the problem has more to do with our need to garner increased critical attention for indigenous artists. I would call for an opening up rather than a narrowing down, for a genuine embrace of heterogeneity and multiple experiences and perspectives. I would resist anything that feels prescribed or reductive.

Best moment: in response to Boris Groys's interpretation of the meaning of curating as fundamentally *curing*, Gerardo Mosquera added that curators are also *caretakers* "who make love to art."

HARRY FONSECA
(Nisenan Maidu / Hawaiian / Portuguese), artist

With the magic of Venice surrounding me, it was somewhat difficult to attend *Where Art Worlds Meet: Multiple Modernities and the Global Salon*, but I did manage. The conference was interesting from the start. To begin with, one could tell that we were looking at and listening to some of the "major" curators, artists, and academics of the so-called mainstream art world. A number had put themselves on metaphorical pedestals and were, as one artist said, "talking around us and not to us, as if we artists were not there." So with that in mind, I sat there for the next few days, listening to the panelists talk about the Venice Biennale and the art world.

I found the subject of the centering and de-centering of art to be an ironic point of departure since we, as Native artists, have been quite conscious of this idea for more than thirty years. Many artists realize that the "mainstream" is actually a trickle when compared to all the art that is being produced around the world. Attempting to capture and document this flow of art in one exhibition is like trying to catch a flock of pigeons with one hand.

What did I learn at this conference? It seems that in the art world there is no agreement about what is or is not accepted as fine art, happening art, hot art, major art, important art, etc. As ever, art history and art criticism are major academic fields of play with their own rules, regulations, teams, and cheering sections. And more often than not, the artist is not invited onto the playing field. As things now stand in regard to an artist "making it," an artist has to wear the right uniform, the artwork has to "look right," and the artist has to be connected somehow to the mainstream art world or be a wild, political person who shocks. Phrases such as "sense of place" or "global salon" are validated as concepts that serve the art world, not the art *in* the world or the artist. The mainstream art world tends to dictate the direction art takes perhaps because the artist allows this to happen.

I think that it was good for the panelists to get feedback from the audience. Alas, I also think it is not going to change the leopard's spots. These professionals have worked very hard indeed for the positions they hold. Despite disagreement about what should be included in a discussion of the art canon, the art world portrayed in this conference has become rigid, exclusive, and limited in its overall vision. I do not believe that this professional rhetoric by experts is anything new; I can hear a group of cavemen saying, "Enok, your art is just inappropriate for this cave!" It has taken a good deal of time and effort to develop these corporate and elevated stances in the art world, and I doubt I can really do anything to change it. The system certainly cares less about what I think. I do not have to believe what I am told, however, and I can move beyond the narrow frame of mind that feeds the mainstream and know that art is alive and moving all the time. We can look at art and the world of art with a wider and more embracing vision.

As an artist, I experienced this conference from a very different point of view. I have been painting most of my life, and I have seen styles come and go. What is "in" usually is "out" sooner rather than later. And to give passing fancy the amount of attention it receives from art magazines, conferences, lectures and such reminds me of fashion. And, of course, this is just the tip of the iceberg in a discussion about the place of art in our society.

I appreciated the opportunity to see old friends, meet new artists, give my input, and be a part of the larger, concerned group that comprised the *Vision, Space, Desire: Global Perspectives and Cultural Hybridity* symposium.

Jeffrey Gibson (*Cherokee/Choctaw*), *artist*

The experience of traveling to Venice for the *Vision, Space, Desire* symposium conjured an array of emotions and excitement about the present and the future. For the first time, I was among a group of peers who shared similar interests in contemporary culture and who allowed the rigid boundaries of what has popularly defined "Native" to loosen and unravel.

After leaving Venice, I returned to my home in Brooklyn only briefly before departing to visit my grandmother in Mississippi. I assumed that these three locations would have nothing to do with each other. As I write, I realize that the combination was a perfect one.

It takes nearly the same amount of time for me to travel from Brooklyn to the Choctaw reservation as it takes to get to Venice. I have traveled back and forth since I was a child. When I was very young, I remember feeling embarrassed about some of the conditions on the reservation. It did not have the superficial glitz and commotion of the cities in which I grew up. My most vivid memory of visiting Mississippi is listening to my grandfather preach and hearing the congregation sing in Choctaw. My grandfather would teach me a few Choctaw words and laugh at me when I would try to complete a sentence. I recall the pine trees—lots and lots of pine trees lining the small highways and filling the reservation. I also remember the first time that I realized what it felt like to be among other people who looked like me. I could see my nose, forehead, eyes, and skin tone reflected back at me as I spoke to other Choctaws. Whenever I left Mississippi, I felt a sense of relief that I was returning to what I knew, the city.

In the city, I would claim that my race did not matter, that my achievements would determine how people saw me. If I worked hard enough, I believed, I could achieve whatever success was dangled in front of me. Still, Mississippi and Oklahoma (where my mother is from) have always remained as very special places. Both continued to challenge the ideas I held about my identity.

When I visited Mississippi this time, though, just after leaving Venice, I saw things differently. My tribe has a successful casino on the reservation; a surreal change from all the pine trees that used to be there. A Hard Rock Cafe, fake beach complete with waves, new spa treatment center, two hotels, two casinos, gourmet restaurant, and valet service await when you arrive. I looked out the window of my eighth-floor hotel room and wondered what the reservation will look like in twenty years or more. Will the casino still be around? How many members will we be? Will the reservation become like the rest of America and blend into suburbia? These are very big questions, I thought, and I am just an artist.

The combination of hearing the opinions expressed during the symposium in Venice and visiting Mississippi just afterward triggered something inside of me that I have not quite figured out yet. I think I am fearful because it is a daunting challenge to even begin to believe that we, the Native people, will help to shape the future of global culture. But I have chosen to believe it. We have gone through far too many generations of Native artists and thinkers who were pushed to the periphery of culture as they pursued what they believed in, created what they desired.

Vision, Space, Desire made me realize that pursuing the success dangled in front of me as a child came at the cost of removing, from my core self, anything that made me different. When I stared out of the window in Mississippi and gazed at the land, I saw all of the things that make me different— and, for the first time, they made me feel stronger and more able to take part in shaping a future. The group of artists, scholars, curators, and writers at the symposium reminded me that I am one small part of a massive collaboration to ensure that our collective voice grows louder and is published more, and that our art is exhibited more, on and off the reservation.

HOCK E AYE VI Edgar Heap of Birds
(Cheyenne/Arapaho), artist

AWAKEN

Artists observe and comment through creation and grow via visual learnings. Our role is also to act as mentors who support artistic endeavors and provide guidance. The artist produces works that become offerings for the betterment of the natural world, loved ones, faraway peoples, and the self.

Our sources and responsibilities of family, partner, and tribe are at once essences that inspire invention and presences to be cared for just as any parent across this broad and diverse society would love child or grandmother. We take in all that we can carry and seek the blessing of knowing our best efforts are meeting these challenges.

In this innovative life path, a prime duty is one that serves the nation of which we are members. This allegiance precedes us from history and extends beyond us. Like tribal soldiers, we will nurture all that is dear and preserve sacred traditions with ceremonial sacrifice, prayer, and song.

Yet as artistic souls striving to maintain indigenous priorities through many actions, we must also give attention to the autonomy of the individual, independent persona. Important space must be allowed for private mind and body. One may revel in an open investigation of self.

From this center of personal spirit and tribal circle, Native artists seek to reach out and commune with the larger world. We desire to speak of ourselves, asking listeners for empathy and respect, and to learn from those with whom we converse. In tribal traditions, we as ceremonial apprentices strive to gain knowledge from a learned person. We approach the elder and ask for this same type of understanding. The elder only responds once a like respect and compassion is offered to him or her. Similarly, in the wider world the learning road is one of a true exchange. To give before taking is an honorable exchange.

The overall success of Native artists lies in viewing creative brothers and sisters from throughout the world as allies. Whether non-Native or tribal, we all suffer and triumph together as artists. Across racial divides, we share more commonalities than differences. Native artists will benefit from contributing their supportive care toward all members of a broad artistic world. Mutual respect will flourish from this exchange. We cannot wait any longer to awaken and dance the circles of participation over the four corners of this earth.

SHANNA KETCHUM *(Navajo), art historian and critic*

TRANSGRESSING THE "NATIONAL": METAPHORS OF EMANCIPATION

The contemporary Native American art scene recently engaged its diametrically opposed constituent (the "mainstream") on the international art front in a move that sought to challenge the latter's penchant for a narrow conception of global cultural relations. With multiculturalist rhetoric serving as the complex backdrop for aspirations and desires, the boundaries between and among these two communities marked and constructed the differences that continue to pervade their relation to one another. As a highly visible social and cultural institution, la Biennale di Venezia provided a site whereby its exclusionary practices could be examined and critically reevaluated, in an intellectual project, to highlight Native American artistic and curatorial practices in the United States and abroad. What seemed to be at stake, considering the titles of both symposiums, *Where Art Worlds Meet: Multiple Modernities and the Global Salon* (headed by Robert Storr, incoming director for the 2007 Venice Biennale) and *Vision, Space, Desire: Global Perspectives and Cultural Hybridity*, organized by the National Museum of the American Indian (NMAI), were issues of cultural production and the relations of power that determine meaning and, to a large extent, exchange value. A sense of displacement permeated the meeting grounds—an international venue that required travel from most of its participants—and forged a politics of space that often accompanies the process of globalization and informs international relations.

Native America's migration toward the international, as signaled by NMAI's endeavors at the Biennale, can be seen as a form of global social criticism[1] in its efforts to locate culturally hybrid art forms within and beyond its own social and cultural spheres or traditions. In this way, we begin to see *culture*, in hybrid terms, as open-ended and constantly reimagined in a space where border identities are transgressed in order to pave the way toward renewed concepts and cultural transformations. In fact, the achievement of a non-Eurocentric conceptualization of multicultural relations depends upon a critical engagement with structural inequalities if the risks of homogenization of Native American experiences are to be overcome. To be sure, this collective effort to move beyond the local, or national, engenders a space of colonial encounter, known as the "contact zone," where knowledge of and action toward "the other" have historically translated into convictions of inferiority and assimilation of subordinated cultures.[2] This comparativist stance toward "the other" privileges one's own cultural categories and denies the internal multiplicity of the hybrid in a process that empowers the imperial and impedes critical self-reflection. Todorov defines this ethnological moment as a "double movement" in which the possibility of recognizing "the other" as both different *and* equal is precluded at the outset. For scholar Jean Fisher, it describes the West's failure to engage in a dialogue of equality and relinquish its control over meaning production as it constantly re-centers itself as the privileged subject of knowledge.[3]

Critical engagement with the "mainstream" thus entails a rereading of hybridity as a space in and through which Natives can voice their own subjectivity by locating their cultural poetics as a politics that calls into question structural inequalities within the art world. This intervention would mean foregoing any desire to measure success in terms of recognition of and by the "mainstream" so that risks of the "double movement" of which Todorov speaks would be deflected. In fact, this typical response to domination describes an effort by the subordinated person to establish mutual relationships in a contact zone where recovery of the self often means a simultaneous loss of the self. Scholar Geeta Kapur questions this method of engaging the mainstream because even if the center-periphery model is turned inside out, the positions might change but the model that keeps it in place would not.[4] Instead, a dialogue that contributes to the reciprocal illumination of one culture by the other is needed from both sides. Not only does this stance offer a way to negotiate the psychology of colonialism inherent to the contact zone, where hierarchies are invoked for domination, but it also situates the Native American subject as an effective agent employing a politics of resistance that avoids assimilation and cultivates self-worth.

In fact, a redefinition of cultural hybridity at home is essential to the critical project because the Native American experience in the United States is still shaped by mythical, nationalistic discourse conceding a substantial amount of historical amnesia concerning its relationship to indigenous populations. It is a condition whereby cultural hybridity is theorized as a metaphor for national sovereignty as differences become reified and power and social inequalities erased, thereby limiting the potential of hybrid social forms and movements to seriously challenge structural inequalities. Indeed, what becomes germane to the discussion, in the quest for visibility on the international art scene, is that one's own reading of the colonial character of the contact zone informs the efforts made toward reimagining one's own relationship to the mainstream. When this stance is taken and deployed as a challenge to neo-colonial oppression both at home and abroad, the contact zone ceases to engender the will to dominate and, instead, offers a vision of liberation for all those involved.

NOTES

1. The term "global social criticism" is used in terms of international theory's use of a postcolonial approach toward international relations. See Naeem Inayatullah and David L. Blaney, *International Relations and the Problem of Difference* (New York and London: Routledge, 2004).

2. This construction of the relation of self to other is discussed by Tzvetan Todorov, foreword by Anthony Pagden, in *The Conquest of America: The Question of the Other* (Norman: University of Oklahoma, 1999).

3. Jean Fisher, "Editor's Note," *Global Visions: Towards a New Internationalism in the Visual Arts* (London: Kala Press, 1994), x–xiv.

4. Geeta Kapur, "A New Inter Nationalism: The Missing Hyphen," in Jean Fisher, ed., *Global Visions: Towards a New Internationalism in the Visual Arts* (London: Kala Press, 1994), 39–49.

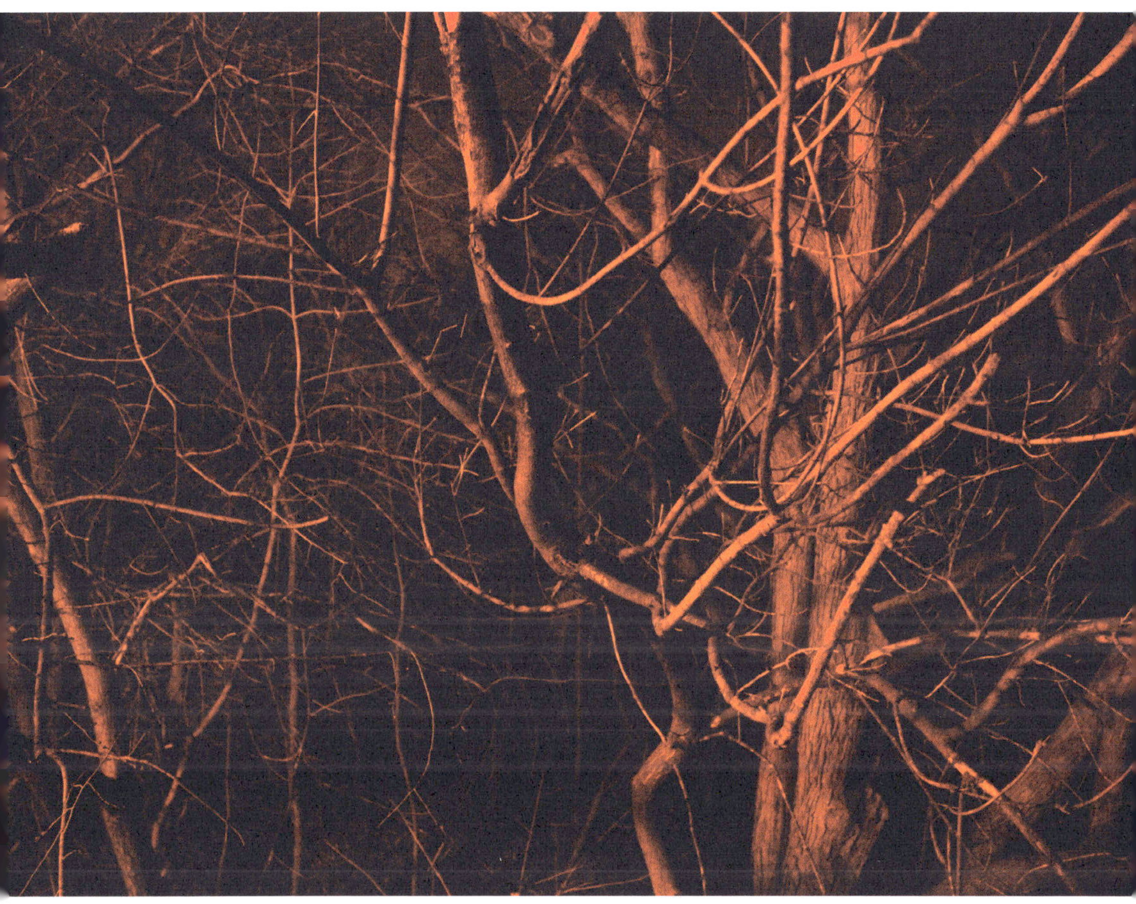

Jason Lujan (Chiricahua Apache, b. 1971), *From One Dream to Another*, 2006.
Film still from DVD, 2 min. © Jason Lujan.

Reflections on Vision, Space, Desire
by Jason Lujan

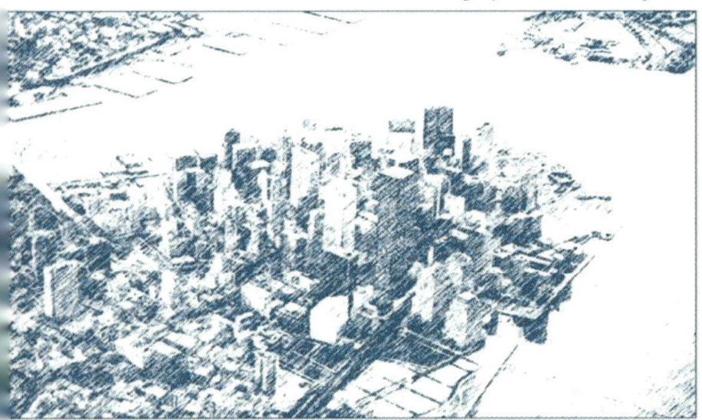

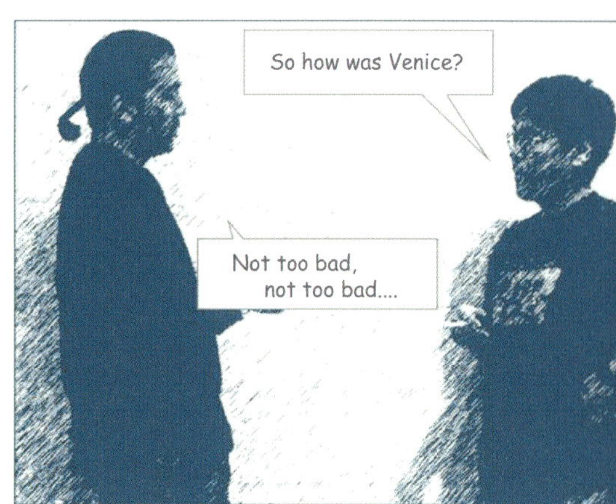

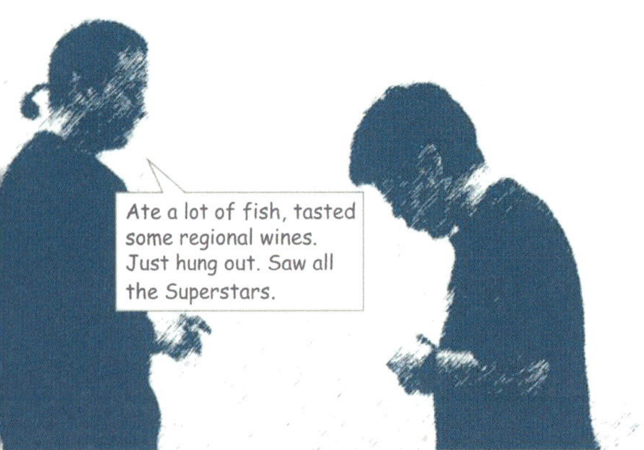

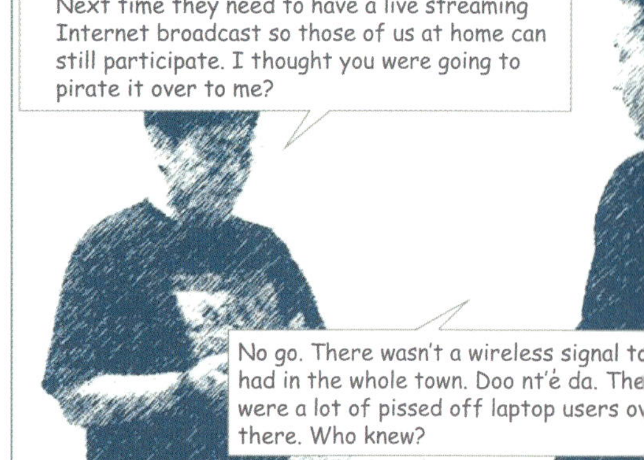

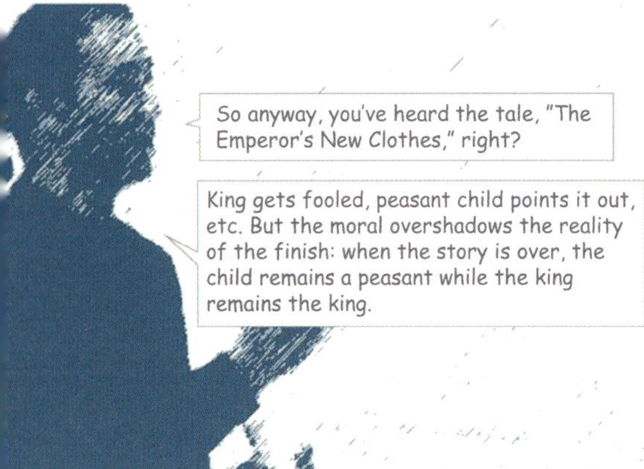

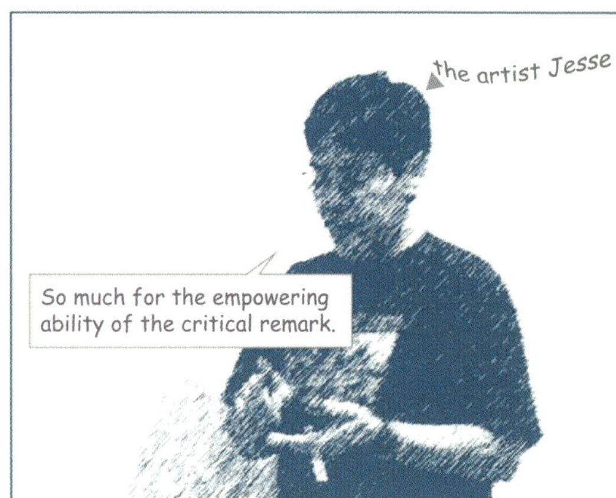

Anyway, it was great; all those artists. The quiet. The red tile roofs. Pigeons.

But those entrenched art apparatchiks.... They bitch and moan but you can see the fear in their eyes. They're scared to death The System is changing and they'll no longer be called upon to hold court, like irrelevant Italian manifesto writers. Once [the invented fiction that is] postcolonial studies is shown to be academic triviality, there will be no need for Professional Indians. So sour. Total lack of "Desire," or "Vision."

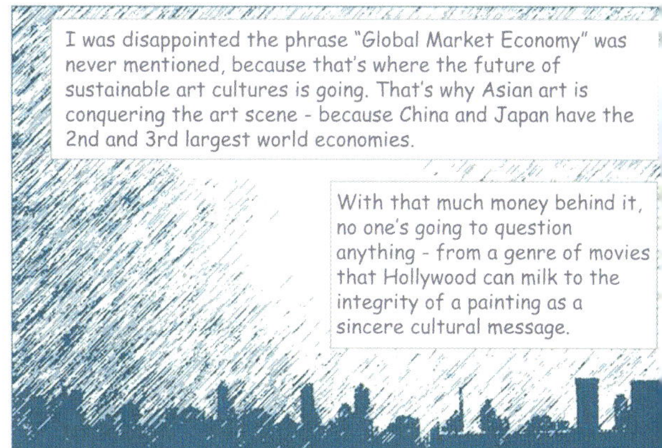

I was disappointed the phrase "Global Market Economy" was never mentioned, because that's where the future of sustainable art cultures is going. That's why Asian art is conquering the art scene - because China and Japan have the 2nd and 3rd largest world economies.

With that much money behind it, no one's going to question anything - from a genre of movies that Hollywood can milk to the integrity of a painting as a sincere cultural message.

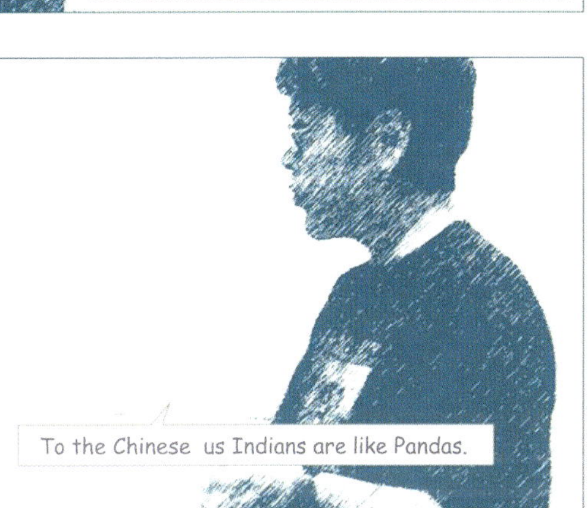

To the Chinese us Indians are like Pandas.

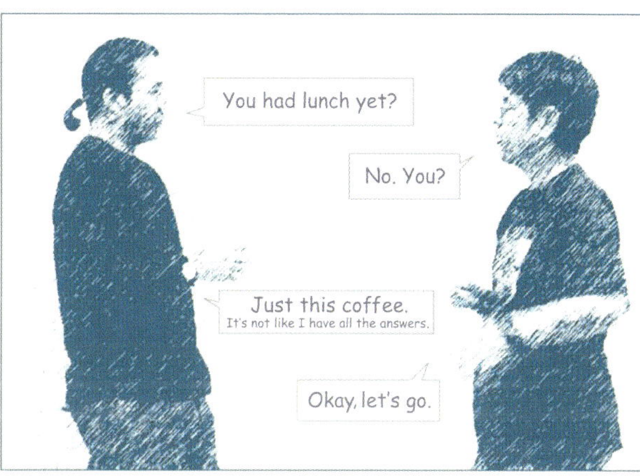

You had lunch yet?

No. You?

Just this coffee.
It's not like I have all the answers.

Okay, let's go.

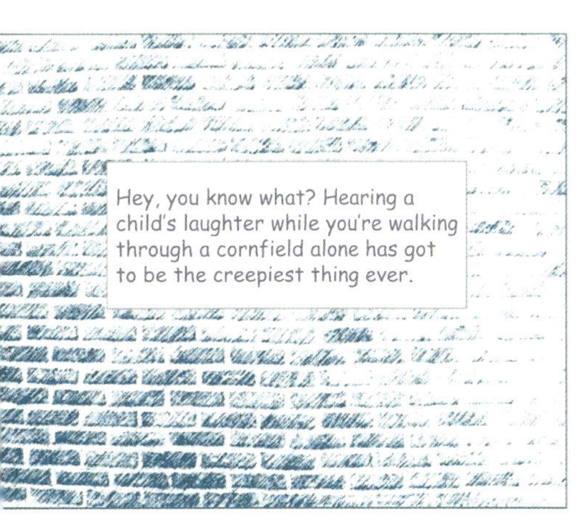

Hey, you know what? Hearing a child's laughter while you're walking through a cornfield alone has got to be the creepiest thing ever.

Adapted from an actual conversation had while standing in front of the AICH Gallery in New York City.

Catherine Mattes (*Métis*), *independent curator*

CONFESSIONS OF A SHAPE-SHIFTING, TIME-TRAVELING, WANNABE B-GIRL[1]

I have a confession to make. At the Biennale and National Museum of the American Indian (NMAI) symposiums, I daydreamed twice during the discussions. These daydreams were not the kind that help you mentally escape from a situation. I was in Venice, after all, having the opportunity to participate in gatherings where art was discussed within a global context. These daydreams were instead responses to some of the discussions that occurred over the five days. They drew on my own work, and involved my "local."

My first daydream happened during the Biennale symposium, when I was finding it to be a bit exclusive and Eurocentric. I couldn't find an entry point into the discussions, even though I found the topics quite relevant. I thought about an opening reception held in 2005 at the Art Gallery of Southwestern Manitoba where I was the curator. The AGSM is located in the small city of Brandon, in the southwest region of Manitoba, Canada. Its mandate includes having at least thirty percent Aboriginal content and developing programming that demonstrates how contemporary art relates to everyday life. My job was to "curate for communities." "Community," of course, is a loaded, ambiguous, and complicated concept.

Calling upon a term I once heard Megan Tamati-Quennell use, I had to be a "shape-shifting time traveler," operating inside and outside of dual contexts, navigating between cultural paradigms, and, at times, being everything to everybody.[2] There were many challenges, failures, and successes at the AGSM, and a lot of risk-taking—practically part of the job description—with the most exciting times being those working with younger adults.

The exhibition celebrated at the opening reception was *Super Phat Nish*, a show of Odawa artist Barry Ace's work that acknowledged and focused on the cultural tenacity of urban Aboriginal youth. Close to three hundred young people, Aboriginal and non-Aboriginal, came. Courtesy of Senate, a local skateboard shop, we had a DJ at the opening, and an after party at a local bar. At Senate's after party, some local artists and I were excitedly dancing on the dance floor. We were elated about the success of the event, because when we were younger, no galleries organized exhibitions for our benefit, and we didn't have artists honoring our cultural tenacity the way that Barry Ace did. As one artist practiced her Michael Jackson moonwalk, I had a hip hop battle with a co-worker. (Everyone said I lost the battle. I disagreed.) In that moment, I was not "Cathy, a curator." I was "Queenie," a shape shiftin', time travellin', hip hop dancing diva, and B-girl extraordinaire! I could navigate across boundaries, relate to artists and communities—and was one fine dancer.

While strutting my stuff, I noticed that none of the young people there would dance. In fact, they were trying hard to keep their distance! At that moment, I was no longer Queenie the extraordinaire. I was that older eccentric arts lady who thought that doing MC Hammer's running man was still cool. At that moment, I was reminded of my "curator-ness." I had not shifted shape as much as I thought.

My other daydream, at the NMAI symposium, took me back to the Métis Youth Arts Gathering, a collaborative effort between the AGSM and the Southwest Métis Youth Centre. The Centre's Youth Network Coordinator Jason Gobeil and I organized a weekend of Métis traditional dance and breakdance workshops that included an excellent artist talk by David Garneau, whose exhibition *Cowboys, Indians (and Métis?)* was showing in the gallery. There was a performance night, where all thirty participants danced for their families and friends. In addition to Métis jigging and breakdancing, the performance included an impromptu salsa lesson in which we invited audience members to join.

During the workshops, as Jason and I ran around frantically, taking our roles as organizers quite seriously, the Skillforce Crew, five breakers[3] leading the breakdance workshops, asked—or should I say dared—me to learn how to do a back handspring. They promised to spot me, and told me not to worry about the concrete floor. A small crowd of participants drew close to watch. Some of them had seemed a little uncertain of themselves during the workshops, and I had been urging them to take risks. I was terrified, but in front of the youth I could not back down.

I'm proud to say, that with the aid of the breakers, I did a back handspring. My knees shook, and I could barely move for a week afterward. It was worth it, though, as the young participants applauded. Instead of just telling them to take chances, I showed them that with a few good spotters supporting you (risk-taking should not equate to total carelessness!) risk-taking has benefits.

During this daydream, I had an epiphany. I finally realized that it was those youth who taught *me* how to take risks. They showed me that to have communities engage with art, you must take every measure necessary to engage with community. This may include back handsprings and salsa dancing.

In my daydream, some of the participants from the Métis Youth Arts Gathering were in Venice. After James Luna had completed his prophetic presentation, some felt compelled to breakdance in his honor. Others, more interested in Métis traditional dance, got up, gave Métis sashes to everyone, and did the Red River Jig. Some, who during the symposium had been quietly listening while drawing their thoughts in graffiti format, gave their art to their favorite speakers. These drawings expressed their opinions of what it means to be Aboriginal and to exist in local and global contexts. One young man began fusing together his breakdance and Métis jigging moves, bringing past, present, and future together.

The young people then insisted that everyone—speakers and audience members alike—dance with them. Breakdance, hip hop, jig, or even salsa, it was one's own choice. But everyone must dance with them. Just as they had danced on their own turf in Brandon, Manitoba, in my daydream they danced in Venice. Venice was now their turf as well. They were fierce; there were no wannabes here. At that moment, as we danced, we were all the ultimate shape-shifting time travelers. And for a brief moment, I was once again "Quee-nie," a shape-shifting, time-traveling, hip hop dancing diva and B-girl extra-ordinaire.[4]

NOTES

1. "B-Girl" is the term for a female breakdancer.

2. Megan Tamati-Quennell, "Shape Shifting Time Travellers," in *Making a Noise, Aboriginal Perspectives on Art, Art History, Critical Writing and Community* (Banff, Alberta: The Banff International Curatorial Institute, 2003), 172–73.

3. "Breakers" is another term for breakdancers.

4. This paper was inspired by two events. The first, a great conversation I had over lunch during the symposiums with Harry Fonseca, Candace Hopkins, and Gerald McMaster about "curating for community." The second, having Harry Fonseca ask me to jig for him in the streets of Venice. Thank you to these three for inspiring this paper.

Alan Michelson *(Mohawk), artist*

FAILURE TO LAUNCH

"Failure to launch." I recently encountered this phrase, twice in the same week. The first was in an article about a new television show starring Heather Graham that was cancelled after only one episode. Network executives had used the expression to justify their decision, and the author of the article disliked the phrase for its distancing from any accountability for the apparent magnitude of the flop. In other words, the people working on the show didn't royally screw up, *the show failed to launch.* I saw these words a second time on a movie poster advertising a romantic comedy with Matthew Mc-Conaughey and Sarah Jessica Parker titled *Failure to Launch.* The tag line was: "To leave the nest, some men need a little push."

Failure to Lunch

Some of the challenges facing contemporary Native artists have little to do with ethnicity; they are those of art and career. To make art, artists need vision, imagination, skill, and materials. To make careers, artists need a cadre of non-artists—curators, dealers, collectors, critics, art administrators, and staffs—to recognize, exhibit, and promote their work. As demonstrated in Venice, this cadre—though tokenly diverse—tends to be white. The contemporary art world relies upon a global radar system apparently unable to detect Native artists (at least in this hemisphere). To many contemporary Native artists, curators, and supporters, this is a vexing issue.

Is the system hopelessly rigged or could contemporary Native artists be flying too low for detection? Are Native artists meeting the vaunted requirements for inclusion? Are they currently equipped to meet them? Most artists know that breaking into this hypercompetitive industry in any of its global manifestations takes more than compelling artwork and luck and are aware of its additional requisites. These boil down to marketing—networking, self-promotion, packaging—and present a huge challenge for artists outside the mainstream. Better strategic marketing on the part of artists as well as better strategic patronage on the part of institutions are needed if we are to compete.

Post-Venice Quiz

How many contemporary Native artists have been included in international biennales since the Columbus Quincentennial in 1992?

How many times has the same Native artist(s) been tapped for these shows?

How many contemporary Native artists are represented by major galleries?

How many contemporary Native artists are represented in major collections?

How many curators in major contemporary art institutions are Native? How many contemporary art critics and historians?

How many reviews of contemporary Native artists have appeared in major art magazines or journals this year?

How many listings of contemporary Native art shows appeared in major magazines, including weekly entertainment publications?

How many New York magazines that routinely list both the historical and contemporary exhibitions of ethnically- or nationally-defined museums like the New York Asia Society and Museum or the Jewish Museum list only the historical shows of the National Museum of the American Indian?

Here is a short list of artists who emerged in the nineties: Fred Wilson, Glenn Ligon, Lorna Simpson, Renée Green, Gary Simmons, Kara Walker, Leonardo Drew, Kerry James Marshall, Jimmie Durham. How many of them are Native?

(For correct answers, conduct study.)

Post-Conference Affirmations

It is advisable not only to have vision but also the means to realize it.

It is advisable not only to make good art but also to make a decent career.

It is advisable not only to perform but also to be accountable for performance.

It is advisable not only to "support" contemporary Native art but also to invest in it.

It is advisable not only to mount contemporary exhibitions but also to market them.

It is advisable not only to produce invitations and catalogues but also to produce ones that meet contemporary standards for content, design, and printing.

It is advisable not only to write catalogue essays but also to write substantial, insightful ones focused on the art.

It is advisable not only to select the best artists for high-profile venues but also to exhibit their best work.

It is advisable to have more Native contemporary art curators, critics, and historians.

It is advisable not only to have boards, donors, and members but also to have those who support contemporary art.

It is advisable not only to have cultural leaders but also ones who can provide real vision, management, and results.

It is advisable not only to hold symposia but also to hold them at a standard as high as that of *Vision, Space, Desire*.

It is advisable to work together in solidarity.

Jaune Quick-to-See Smith
(Enrolled Flathead Salish, Member of the Confederated Salish and Kootenai Nation of Montana), artist

Contemporary Native painters, sculptors, performance/installation artists, photographers, and videographers are some of today's most original, powerful, and groundbreaking artists in the whole of the United States as well as the Native community. They are the segue from the traditional world to the cyber world. They are the past and the present. They are the soothsayers, the seers, the tricksters who critique, poke fun, and provide dialogue with the global world. Where is this written?

We, contemporary Native artists, have no major art collectors in our midst, thus there is no interpretive writing as these two endeavors go hand in hand, side by side. With no interpretive monographs acting as ripples from the exhibition pebbles in the mainstream world, our work stays hidden and remains in silence, unempowered and anonymous.

Perhaps the largest single private collection of contemporary Native art is held, not by an American museum or an American collector, but by a German citizen who has traversed the United States to artists' studios biannually for more than twenty years. Dorothee Peiper has an in-depth collection of more than one hundred paintings, sculptures, drawings, and prints. An attendee at the Venice symposium, Peiper stood and gave a spirited comment about the fact that the major New York museums, who have collected Indian pots in the past, do not collect contemporary Indian art nor show it, as opposed to the Canadian museums, which are steadily collecting from contemporary Native artists and showing their work.

Prior to their opening, I encouraged the new National Museum of the American Indian to rectify this neglect of contemporary Native art as one of their first acts of courage in generating change. Again—I repeat myself here—I propose that we mentor our young scholars and document our older artists for the hour is late. Colonial America has controlled and stifled the documentation of our living contemporary Native artists. If our own national Native museum chooses not to "authenticate" contemporary living Native artists, who then will?

For starters, there has never been a major national touring group exhibit of contemporary Native painting and drawing with a catalogue such as Latinos and African Americans have had in recent decades. Perhaps a funding plan is in order, which might be discussed with our casino Indians who need to hear about the severity of this situation and how to remedy it.

If we want to compete in the global world, we Native people must take certain steps that enlist recognition, respect, and acknowledgment in order to empower ourselves. For if we are not doing this for ourselves, how can we expect others to join us in forging these alliances? By not being proactive, we marginalize ourselves.

With interpretive writing will come respected collections both by private collectors and public museums. Today, there is not one major collection of contemporary Native art in this country by any private collector or public museum. By "major," I mean three hundred to five hundred pieces or more. There are major collections in this country that contain several hundred pieces by Caribbean artists, Haitian artists, Cuban artists, outsider artists, women artists, black artists, Mexican artists, Latin American artists, and religious artists, to name only a few.

I am sad to report that beyond the long-time collecting of craft by white colonial collectors and institutions, there has been no in-depth collecting of Native artists born in the 1930s, '40s and '50s who are today's aging generations. We share conversations about where our work will go upon our deaths, and we offer vague comments that perhaps a museum will contact our children or grandchildren in the future.

I am in anguish over this dilemma and the forgotten generations of America's First Peoples. There will be a big hole where this history should reside—its art and its documentation instead in a sidelined limbo and not a part of the larger art world. This affects not only Native America and not only United States art history but also the whole of American history.

LORETTA SARAH TODD *(Métis/Cree)*,
film director and writer

A FEW DAYS IN DECEMBER IN VENICE

On 670 hectares of surface, resting on millions of petrified wood pilings pounded into the bottom of the *laguna,* rests Venice. Here about 70,000 residents occupy a statistical average of 1,000 square feet each. If you add the tourists, in any given month, the population is about double, giving each 500 square feet.

I went to Venice to occupy my 500 square feet—more than the square footage of the apartments most indigenous people occupy in Vancouver where I live. In fact, there are many homeless in Vancouver—in Canada, for that matter—who have no roof over their heads, let alone square footage.

There is a move of late to imagine Vancouver as the new Venice—a place of commerce, culture, and ideas. I wonder what that means for Vancouver and the people who live here and the land we occupy? Can Vancouver be the new Venice?

In the old Venice, merchants held sway and knew with certainty the Doge could be counted on to do what was needed to maintain their wealth. (I wander the rooms of the Doge's Palace and see imagery of war and commerce intersecting.)

In Vancouver, merchants will benefit from billions going toward the 2010 Winter Olympics. In old Venice, patrician merchants with political privileges financed an engineering marvel that endures today as a UNESCO

World Heritage Site. In Vancouver—the "new" Venice—after the Olympics, there will be curling rinks and roads to ski hills where martini-sipping swingers will go to party—and still more homeless.

But this is about Venice, not about Vancouver. Or more, it is about *Vision, Space, Desire: Global Perspectives and Cultural Hybridity.*

I think of Venice—the space, and Venice—the desire. That is, the desire artists and filmmakers have to be vetted and venerated at biennales, festivals, and symposiums in Venice. This Venice is imaginary. It is where artists imagine being imagined.

First, I attend the Biennale's event, *Where Art Worlds Meet: Multiple Modernities and the Global Salon.* On a panel, former Biennale artists have little good to say about being at the Biennale. Or so it seems. Perhaps they behave as is expected of them. That is, to be indifferent to their success—because they are, after all, artists.

Besides, for some, success is a genuine distraction—though it feels good in cashmere. The artists in the audience offer timid response—wondering if business and art must merge. Perhaps the subtext is: ungrateful Venice Biennale artists.

(When I get home, I give the *Where Art Worlds Meet* conference bag to my brother who is a great painter—but given the odds, unlikely to be curated at the Venice Biennale. Later, I wonder if he has one of those "My sister went to the Venice Biennale *Where Art Worlds Meet: Multiple Modernities and the Global Salon,* and all I got was this plastic bag" moments.)

Vision, Space, Desire happens after the Biennale event, though they are linked. The presenters are all brilliant, thoughtful, and generous with their knowledge. The speakers stimulate my vision and my desire for more discussion.

I'm struck by the fearlessness of James Luna and Rebecca Belmore—at the symposium and in their art. James Luna narrates some of Jimi Hendrix's story, weaving Hendrix with his own experience at the Venice Biennale. Where do we have to go to get noticed?—because artists—yes, including indigenous artists—want to be noticed. Who do you have to be to get noticed?

Everyone from the symposium leaves, and I stay in Venice for a few days. I encounter the in-between space of Venice: neither city nor state, neither sea nor land—yet sacred and secular, decadent and chaste. Venice—once empire and now a global market of art.

Sitting in a café, I recall the exchange I had in *Where Art Worlds Meet* when I questioned the failure of materialism. Yes, I guess I'm a good materialist, but I function within a world where you can be both a materialist and meta-physical. I question the almost "gleeful" use of the term "cannibalism" by some presenters. I get its theoretical context, but if there are "different ways of being different"—then I can be frustrated by its use. But that isn't what really troubles me so much.

Though I craved the ideas in the symposiums, there is a sneaking feeling that we are covering the same ground. They call it the static present—pre-sentness. Not so much the end of history as the persistence of now.

Yes, I get that "aesthetic standardization" thing, of how art can be too easy for certain classes to experience without trying. Yes, art must frustrate consumption—to paraphrase Boris Groys, who offers how at the exhibition the "visitor's judgement" should be "subverted" creating insecurity—forc-ing a critical engagement.

James Luna and Rebecca Belmore do just that—force visitors to be in-secure in their notions about "Indians." Yet, it isn't forcing frustration for frustration's sake—it is the result of Luna's and Belmore's aesthetic state-ments—told through their performance art, engaged with their political, cultural, personal, multidimensional human selves. There is no such thing as the end of "Indian" history in their work (though there may be the end of certain histories of "Indianness"). Nor is there a sense of catching up to the static present. Instead there is energy, change, and movement, made tactile and physical in Belmore, made gestural and verbal in Luna.

So, I examine Boris Groys's response to my comments about the failure of materialism during the *Centering and Decentering Subjects of Art* panel. I offer another perception—that you can experience the infinite, and cannibalism is an admission of the finiteness, the limits of materialism. He says it is self-deception and dangerous to think that the infinite can be experienced/ex-pressed in infinite terms. Another panelist, Salah Hassan, opens the possi-bility of other knowledge systems.

I'm not sure if I'm being dissed by Groys (not personally, of course) because of the infinite reference, the materialism reference, or because I brought up spirituality. But I also understand the reaction. Typically, as soon as "indigenous" or "tribal" people bring up the spiritual, they are marginalized in a room full of materialists—even looked upon as quaint.

I think good materialists should engage in self-criticism—and not just regarding degrees of critical theory and schools of philosophy or art history—but with regard to the nature of knowledge and, if nothing else, with regard to what is dismissed as essentialism in Native art theories and philosophies. And we as indigenous intellectuals and artists must examine our relationship to our concepts of essentialism as a site of resistance and our metaphysical selves within our knowledge systems.

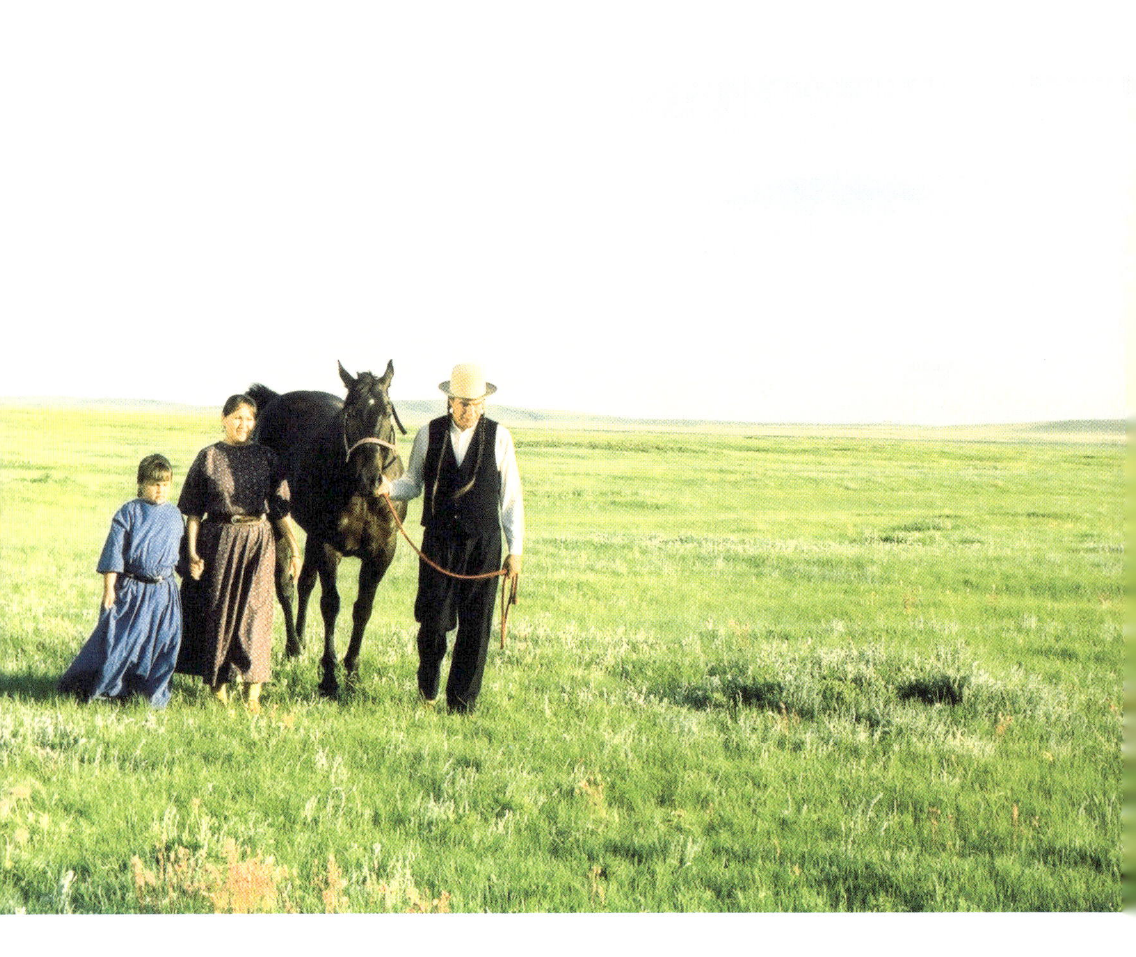

Kainayssini Imanistaisiwa: The People Go On. Directed and written by Loretta Todd (Métis/Cree). Still by Morton Molyneux. © 2003 National Film Board of Canada.